DO YOUR OWN
DRYWALL
AN ILLUSTRATED GUIDE

FOR MIKE
Thanks for everything
You helped me with this
much more than you know

No. 1838
$17.95

DO YOUR OWN
DRYWALL
AN ILLUSTRATED GUIDE

A.J. KOZLOSKI

TAB BOOKS Inc.
Blue Ridge Summit, PA 17214

Although all possible measures have been taken to ensure
the accuracy of the material presented, neither the author nor
TAB BOOKS Inc. is liable in case of misinterpretation of
directions, misapplication, or typographical error.

FIRST EDITION

FIRST PRINTING

Copyright © 1985 by TAB BOOKS Inc.
Printed in the United States of America

Library of Congress Cataloging in Publication Data

Kozloski, Arnold.
Do your own drywall.

Includes index.
1. Dry wall—Amateurs' manuals.   I. Title.
TH2239.K69   1985   690'.12   84-23990
ISBN 0-8306-0838-9
ISBN 0-8306-1838-4 (pbk.)

Contents

Acknowledgments   **vii**

Introduction   **viii**

1   Drywall Materials   **1**
Gypsum Wallboard—Joint Compounds—Joint Reinforcements—Gypsum Wallboard Fasteners

2   Drywalling Tools   **17**
Cutting Tools—Joint Finishing Tools—Other Useful Tools

3   Drywall Estimating   **33**
Your Time—Gypsum Wallboard Requirements—Fastener Requirements—Joint Reinforcement
Requirements—Joint Compound Requirements—Large Drywalling Projects

4   Gypsum Wallboard Applicaton   **38**
Before You Start—Nailing Gypsum Wallboard—Cutting Gypsum Wallboard—Drywalling the Ceiling—
Drywalling the Walls—Drywalling Curved Surfaces—Reinforcing Corners

5   Joint Finishing   **65**
Before You Start—Handling Joint Knives and Joint Compound—Applying the Filler Coat—Applying the
Second Coat—Applying the Finish Coat

79005

6 Drywall Repairs   **87**
Damaged Wallboard—Defective Drywall Systems

7 Mounting Fixtures   **108**
Installing Spring-Loaded Toggle Bolts—Installing Expanding Wall Anchors—Finding Studs and Joists

8 Textured Ceilings   **115**
Texturing Materials—Texturing Tools—Before You Start—Applying the Texture

9 Building Codes, Permits, and Inspections   **123**
Building Codes—Plumbing Code—Mechanical Code—The National Electrical Code—Building Permits—Building Inspections—Building Inspectors

Appendix   **130**

Glossary   **138**

Index   **145**

Acknowledgments

I would like to thank the people of the following organizations for the information, illustrations, photographs, and materials they so cheerfully provided:

Black & Decker Inc.
701 E. Joppa Road
Towson, MD 21204

Building Department, City of Sierra Vista
2400 Tacoma Avenue
Sierra Vista, AZ 85615

Goldblatt Tool Co.
511 Osage, PO Box 2334
Kansas City, KS 66110

Red Devil Inc.
2400 Vauxhall Road
PO Box 155
Union, NJ 07083

United States Gypsum Company
101 S. Wacker Drive
Chicago, IL 60606

Wallboard Tool Co., Inc.
1708 Seabright Avenue
PO Box 20319
Long Beach, CA 90801

Zircon International Inc.
475 Vandell Avenue
Campbell, CA 95009

Introduction

This book is written for homesteaders and do-it-yourselfers. It covers the areas of drywall construction that are most applicable to residential construction and home improvements in particular. It has been written in the simplest language possible and amplified generously with photos, diagrams, and tables.

The most modern drywall products and materials are introduced and discussed. Special tools that make drywalling easy are also examined carefully. Many hints on estimating and on drywall hanging are presented. The heart of this book is the portion that covers joint-finishing techniques. The methods described in those pages rarely, if ever, receive attention in other construction books.

During my years as a contractor, I found that most of my clients were willing to tackle almost any project except drywalling, mostly due to the anticipated heartache of joint finishing. I learned most of what I know about drywall construction through trial, error, and more error. Once I learned the tricks, drywalling became quite simple. In this book

I have attempted to give you the benefit of my trials and errors.

After reading this book, you should be able to tackle your drywalling projects with confidence. When I first started drywalling, it typically took me seven coats of joint compound to get the joints right. With practice (actually discovery is a better word), I got it down to three coats and eventually two, both of which were applied in the same day. If you follow my instructions carefully, you should be able to do it yourself in three coats the first time. People pay me well to do simple drywalling jobs they could easily do themselves with the aid of a book like this one.

In recent years, drywall construction has become more sophisticated. This is particularly true in the area of large-scale and industrial applications. Many new innovations in the areas of tools and materials have made drywall construction a lucrative undertaking for the contractor. Small-scale, residential drywall construction has remained relatively unchanged, although it has made strides of its own, too. Because this book is for beginners and do-it-yourselfers, I decided not to belabor you with a discussion of industrial practices.

This book would not have been possible without the help of the individuals of the organizations listed in the acknowledgments section. They were very generous in providing me with information, illustrations, and, in some cases, actual products. They will gladly provide additional information to anyone requesting it.

So, because you don't have to learn it all the hard way like I did, go boldly forth and do it yourself.

Chapter 1

Drywall Materials

Gypsum wallboards were first introduced 60 years ago. Their appearance revolutionized interior wall covering. First drywall construction has many advantages over conventional plaster coverage. First, drywall construction with gypsum wallboards is applied in a dry state—hence, the name drywall. No moisture is contributed to the structure during construction, and lengthy drying times are not required as they are with plaster. Therefore, construction can continue during the winter months.

Drywall is less expensive and more easily installed than plaster. The finished wall system is also more easily decorated. Drywall construction contributes significantly less weight to the structure than does plaster. The greatest advantage that drywall offers over other wall coverings is its resistance to fire. In some cases, fire resistance ratings of up to four hours can be achieved using gypsum wallboard.

Gypsum wallboard begins in the ground as a grayish white rock called gypsum. Gypsum is a mineral (calcium sulfate) that contains chemically combined water called water of crystallization. In the finished product, this water constitutes about 20 percent of the wallboard weight. It is this water that gives gypsum wallboard its fire-resistive nature.

Once the gypsum rock is mined, it is crushed and dried. Next, much of the chemically combined water, but not all of it, is driven off as steam through a process called calcination. After that, water and other ingredients are added to the crushed gypsum to form it into a plaster commonly known as plaster of Paris. Then the plaster is sandwiched between two sheets of special paper to create the finished product, the gypsum wallboard. Figure 1-1 shows a modern gypsum wallboard production line.

The most impressive feature of gypsum wallboard is its ability to resist fire. Gypsum wallboards start as rocks in the ground. Rocks don't burn all that well and neither do the wallboards, but there is more to it than that. When intense heat is applied to a gypsum wallboard, the chemically combined water in the gypsum core is released as steam, which acts as a very effective heat barrier.

Fig. 1-1. A modern gypsum wallboard production facility (courtesy of the United States Gypsum Company).

The steam carries away heat as it evaporates. This is actually the process of calcination repeating itself.

When the surface of a gypsum wallboard is exposed to temperatures of 1900° F. The temperature on the other side of the wallboard is only about 900° F. The temperature 2 inches behind the wallboard surface is only 220° F, far below the temperature at which wood ignites.

The calcination process takes about 30 minutes for a standard ¼-inch thick gypsum wallboard. For wallboards with special gypsum cores (called type X wallboard), this time is increased to 45 minutes; for wallboards thicker than ½ inch, it takes 60 minutes.

Fire ratings of up to four hours can be achieved using various construction methods. The Gypsum Association, at 1603 Orrington Avenue, Evanston Illinois 60201, publishes a *Fire Resistance Design Manual* that specifies the fire resistance ratings of various gypsum wallboard assemblies.

GYPSUM WALLBOARD

Over the years, gypsum wallboards have been produced in many types and sizes. You have no doubt heard the name Sheetrock used to describe gypsum wallboards. You might even wonder why this book wasn't titled "Do your own Sheetrock." Sheetrock is a trade name of the United States Gypsum Com-

2

pany and is used properly only in reference to their product.

The most commonly used gypsum wallboard is ½ inch thick, 4 feet wide, and 8 feet long, with a 30-minute fire rating. The standard width of all gypsum wallboards is 4 feet. The length varies from 6 feet to 16 feet. The most popular length is 8 feet, but 12-foot sheets typically cost twice as much as 8-foot sheets for only 50 percent more coverage, the expense is offset by saved labor during joint finishing.

The thickness of gypsum wallboard varies from ¼ inch to ⅝ inch in ⅛-inch increments. The ½-inch thickness is the most popular for residential construction. Generally the thicker the sheet, the greater its resistance to fire and sound transmission and the less apt it is to sag when installed on a ceiling. Thinner sheets are less expensive, lighter, and can be more easily bent for installation over curved surfaces.

The long edges of gypsum wallboards are tapered so that a valley is formed at the adjacent edges of wallboards upon installation. This valley, as shown in Fig. 1-2, allows paper to be buried below the wallboard surface in joint compound during the joint finishing process. Such a joint is very easy to finish. The 4-foot-wide ends of the wallboard are cut squarely without a taper. The joints formed at the wallboard ends, called butt joints, are a little tougher to finish than valley joints. If the wallboards are properly installed, however, the butt joints will only be 4 feet long, making them somewhat easier to finish.

There are other options available in gypsum wallboard with regard to core and covering type. Type X wallboards have increased fire resistance ratings of up to 1 hour and are used where greater flame resistance is needed.

Gypsum wallboards with moisture-resistant backings are used to provide both a wall covering and an effective vapor barrier. Figure 1-3 shows foil-backed panels being applied to furring strips over a masonry wall to retard moisture entry into the room.

Wallboard with water-resistant cores and face papers are designed for areas where plastic or ceramic tile will be applied directly to the wallboard surface, such as in kitchens or bathrooms. Figure 1-4 shows tile being applied to the face of water-resistant gypsum wallboard. Water-resistant wallboards have specially treated and laminated face and backing papers, and an asphalt composition core that together make the wallboard water resistant clear through.

Gypsum wallboards designed for indirect exposure to weather can be used to finish the underside of eaves, soffits, and exterior ceilings such as those in carports and patios. Exterior ceiling boards have a water-repellent paper jacket and a sag-resistant gypsum core. Exterior ceiling boards were used to finish the ceiling shown in Fig. 1-5.

Gypsum panels that are predecorated with vinyl coverings are also available. The edges and joints are trimmed with vinyl trim and molding. Such panels are intended only for interior use. They are fastened with colored nails and are great for constructing movable partitions.

Gypsum wallboards come packaged in pairs that are taped together at the ends. Figure 1-6 shows the tape being removed prior to wallboard application. The wallboards are taped with the finish sides together. The finish side is the side of the wallboard intended for decoration as the finished wall surface. It is also the side with the tapered edge. The finish side is covered with smooth manila paper. The backing side is placed

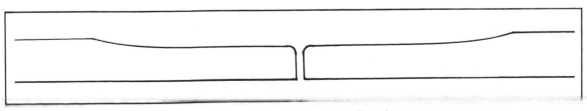

Fig. 1-2. The valley formed by the tapered edges of adjacent gypsum wallboards.

Fig. 1-3. Foil-backed gypsum wallboards being installed over a masonry wall to provide a vapor barrier (courtesy of the United States Gypsum Company).

against the framing members and is covered with coarse, gray paper.

Wallboards are less likely to be damaged if they are left taped together during handling. Nevertheless, they can be a little tough for one person to handle. A single ½-inch, 8-foot wallboard weighs about 58 pounds; a pair will weigh 116 pounds. Type X and water-resistant panels are a bit heavier. A pair of type X water-resistant, ⅝-inch, 4-by-12-foot sheets will weigh 240 pounds. Take a strong friend to the lumberyard with you. Figure 1-7 shows some of the different types of gypsum

Fig. 1-4. Mastic and tile being applied directly to the face of water-resistant gypsum wallboard (courtesy of the United States Gypsum Company).

5

Fig. 1-5. Exterior ceiling board was used to cover this outdoor gypsum ceiling (courtesy of the United States Gypsum Company).

Fig. 1-6. Peeling the tape from the ends of a pair of gypsum wallboards.

Type & Thickness (5)	Core Type				Foil-Back Option	Edge Formation	Lengths (ft.)(mm)				
	(1) Reg.	(2) FC	(3) FC "C"	(4) Asphlt			8 2448	9 2745	10 3050	12 3660	14 4265
SHEETROCK Brand Reg. Panels											
1/4"	X					Tapered	X		X		
3/8"	X				X	Tapered	X	X	X	X	X
1/2"	X		X		X	Tapered	X	X	X	X	X
5/8"	X	X	X		X	Tapered	X	X	X	X	X
SHEETROCK Brand W/R Panels											
1/2"			X(4)	X		Tapered	X	X	X	X	
5/8"			X(4)	X		Tapered	X	X	X	X	
Exterior Ceiling Board											
1/2"	X					Tapered and Eased	X			X	
5/8"	X	X				Tapered and Eased	X			X	
TEXTONE Panels											
1/2"	X		X			Beveled	X	X	X		
5/8"	X	X	X			Beveled	X	X	X		
USG Gypsum Sheathing											
1/2"				X		V-T&G(6)	X				
1/2"				X		Square	X	X			
5/8"			X(4)	X		Square	X	X			
USG Triple-Sealed Gypsum Sheathing											
4/10"	X					Square	X	X			
GYP-LAP Gypsum Sheathing											
1/2"	X					V-T&G(6) Square	X X				
5/8" *											

(1) Regular. (2) FIRECODE. (3) FIRECODE "C" (4) Asphalted. (5) All boards 4-ft (1219 mm) width (except USG Sheathing 2 & 4-ft. (610 & 1219 mm) widths); (6) In 2-ft. (610 mm) width only; 4-ft (1219 mm) width has square edges
*Available upon special request.

Fig. 1-7. Some of the different types of gypsum wallboard available from one manufacturer (courtesy of the United States Gypsum Company).

wallboard available from one manufacturer.

JOINT COMPOUNDS

There are as many different types of drywall joint finishing compounds as there are types of gypsum wallboards. Joint compound has been referred to by a variety of names such as "spackle" or spackling compound, but by far the most common name is "mud." If you go to the lumberyard and ask for a bucket of mud, the guy behind the counter will know exactly what you want.

Drywall joint compound comes in two basic forms: powdered and premixed. Powdered joint compounds must be mixed with water to the proper consistency. Premixed joint compounds are ready to use right out of the bucket. While powdered compounds can be stored just about forever and used a little at a time, I suggest you avoid them. The premixed compounds are ready to go without mixing; there are no lumps, mess, or air bubbles to deal with. I always use premixed mud.

Joint compounds can be further divided into two more categories. These are drying types and hardening types. Hardening compounds have several advantages and drawbacks. Some hardening compounds will cure as quickly as 20 minutes, allowing immediate additional coating or decorating.

The curing time is also unaffected by temperature or humidity. Hardening compounds are well suited for exterior applications. The drawback is that hardening compounds are not easily sanded after they cure. They must be worked to a near-finished state during application. It is for this reason alone that beginners should avoid them. Hardening compounds should only be used by experienced drywallers. Hardening compounds come only in powder form. The addition of water begins the chemical process of hardening.

Drying-type joint compounds come in both powdered and premixed form. Drying compounds are vinyl based and do not contain asbestos (neither do hardening types). As with gypsum, they do not support combustion. They normally require 24 hours drying time between coats and especially before painting. Drying time will vary with temperature, humidity, and thickness of coat. The major advantage of drying compounds is that they are easily applied and easily sanded after they dry. These are very important considerations for the beginning drywaller.

Joint compounds, whether powdered or premixed, hardening or drying, can be divided into three more types. These are taping, topping, and all-purpose joint compounds.

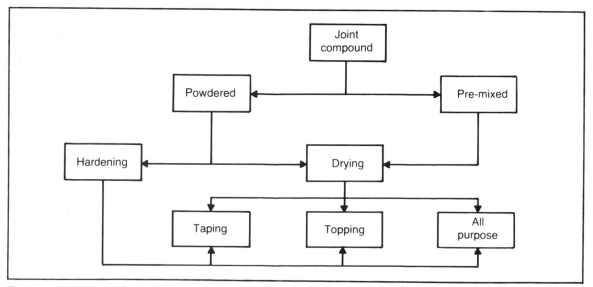

Fig. 1-8. A breakdown of the different types of joint compounds.

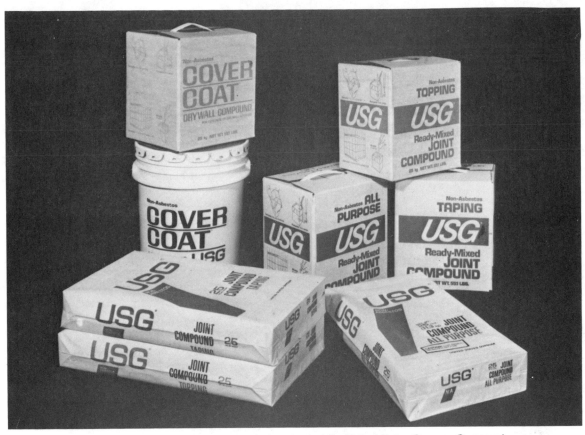

Fig. 1-9. Large containers of various joint compounds (courtesy of the United States Gypsum Company).

Taping compounds are designed for filling joints, embedding joint tape and corner beads, and filling nailheads during first coats. Taping compounds provide superior bonding strength and hardening, but they tend to shrink and crack during drying. Taping compounds are not easily sanded once they dry.

Topping compounds are intended for use in second and third coats over taping or all-purpose joint compounds. Topping compounds provide little structural bonding, but they experience almost no shrinkage during drying. They are also very easily applied and sanded smooth to provide a superior finished surface.

All-purpose joint compounds combine the best features of taping and topping compounds—good bonding, minimal shrinkage and cracking, easy

sanding, and smooth finishing. All-purpose compounds can be used for all coats, from first to last, and are the best choice for the part-time or beginning drywaller. The versatility of all-purpose joint compound makes it economical to use. The beginning drywaller should use premixed, all-purpose joint compound to simplify drywalling projects.

Other special-purpose joint compounds are available for various applications. Water-resistant joint compound is used to finish and seal the joints of water-resistant wallboards, thus enhancing the moisture resistance of the drywall system. Figure 1-8 gives a breakdown of the most common joint compound options available.

Joint compounds can be purchased in a wide variety of packages. The most popular is the 5-gallon (62-pound) bucket. It also comes in boxes of the same size, as can be seen in Fig. 1-9. For most projects other than small repairs, the 5-gallon container is the most economical.

A few examples of smaller containers of joint compound ideally suited for small jobs are shown in Fig. 1-10. Pails of mud from 1 pint to 2 gallons, tubes from 2 to 16 ounces, and caulking gun cartridges from 11 to 29 ounces can be found.

JOINT REINFORCEMENTS

All drywall joints must be reinforced during the joint finishing process to prevent them from cracking in the future. Valley, butt, and inside corner joints are reinforced with paper joint tape. Paper joint tape is normally about 2 inches wide and comes in rolls anywhere from 50 to 500 feet long. A 75-foot roll of joint tape is shown in Fig. 1-11. Note that the joint tape in the figure has a preformed crease down the center. This allows the tape to be easily folded for application to inside corner joints. There is no adhesive on either side of the tape. Bonding is provided by joint compound.

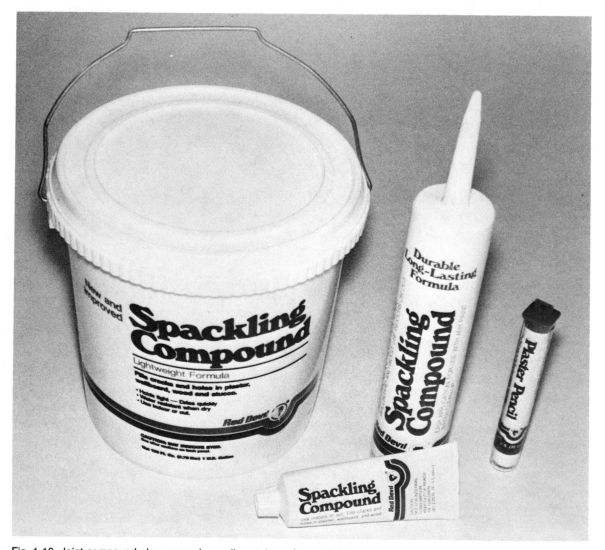

Fig. 1-10. Joint compound also comes in small containers for repair jobs or other small projects.

Fig. 1-11. A 75-foot roll of 2-inch paper joint tape. Note the center crease.

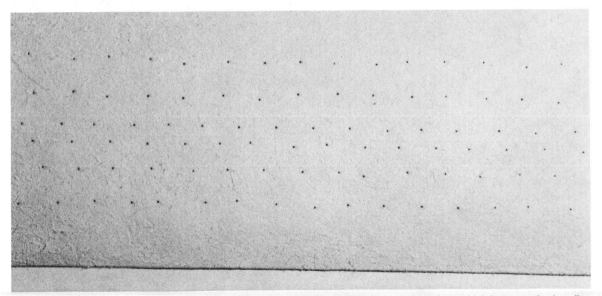

Fig. 1-12. A close-up view of a piece of paper joint tape reveals tiny holes and a rough surface which increase the bonding strength of the tape.

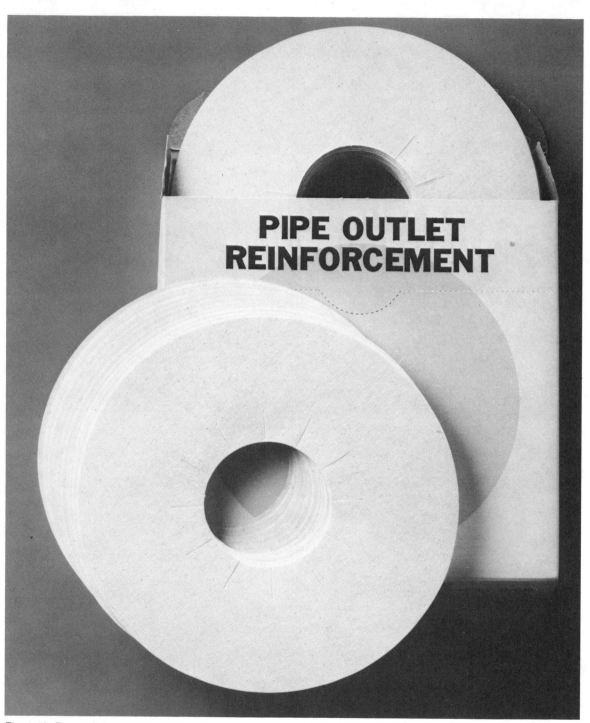

Fig. 1-13. Paper pipe outlet reinforcements (courtesy of Goldblatt Tool Company).

Paper joint tape is made in two forms, with holes and without. The perforated tape is best due to its increased bonding quality. Figure 1-12 illustrates the tiny holes in a piece of perforated joint tape. As you can see, the holes aren't very large. Examine joint tape closely before you purchase it. The surface of the paper is fairly rough to increase bonding. Good joint tape is made from high-fiber paper that resists stretching, thus reducing the chances of the joint cracking.

There are some variations on joint tape for special applications. One of these is the pipe outlet reinforcement shown in Fig. 1-13. It has small holes in it and it is used to reinforce the holes through which pipes pass into rooms, such as a drainpipe under a sink.

Another type of joint tape is shown in Fig. 1-14. It is a paper tape with two metal strips in it. It is called corner tape and can be used to finish butt, valley, inside, and outside corner joints.

The item most commonly used to finish and reinforce outside corners is a galvanized metal corner bead. There are many types (see Fig. 1-15). The use of a corner bead creates a straight and durable corner. The round nose of the bead protects the corner from damage and provides a form for proper filling and finishing of the flanges with joint compound. Figure 1-16 shows the most popular corner beads used in drywall construction.

Generally, the wider the bead flanges the better the joint bonding. Some corner beads are treated with chemical bonding agents that increase

Fig. 1-14. Paper and metal corner tape (courtesy of Goldblatt Tool Company).

13

Fig. 1-15. A wide variety of metal corner beads, channels, and trim (courtesy of the United States Gypsum Company).

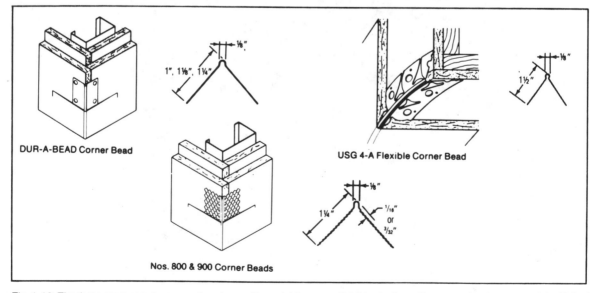

DUR-A-BEAD Corner Bead

USG 4-A Flexible Corner Bead

Nos. 800 & 900 Corner Beads

Fig. 1-16. The three most popular corner beads used for outside corner finishing in drywall construction (courtesy of the United States Gypsum Company).

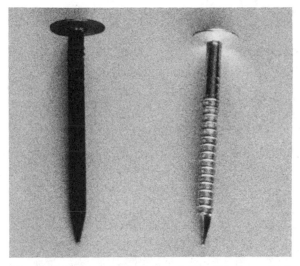

Fig. 1-17. The two basic types of drywall nails, cement-coated and annular-ringed.

their adhesion to joint compounds. Most corner beads come in 7-foot or 8-foot lengths, but others are available.

GYPSUM WALLBOARD FASTENERS

There are three basic ways to fasten gypsum wallboard to the framing members of a structure: with nails, screws, and glue. The beginning drywaller should forget screws. Nails are the most popular, convenient, and economical fastener to use. Drywall nails used along with glue will provide a superior fastening system that retards joint cracking and nail popping in the finished drywall system.

The two types of drywall nails are the annular-ringed and cement-coated nails. I prefer to use the cement-coated nails. They hold as well as the annular-ringed type and seem to drive more easily and resist bending better. Both types are shown in Fig. 1-17.

Drywall nails come in lengths ranging from 1¼ to 2⅛ inches long in ⅛-inch steps. The nailheads are between ¼ to 19/64 of an inch wide. The thickness of drywall nails runs between #12 and #14 American wire gauge. Table 1-1 lists the recommended nail sizes for various wallboard thicknesses. There are generally 300 to 350 drywall nails per pound.

As I said earlier, glue should be used to fasten gypsum wallboards to the studs and joists along with nails. The extra adhesion provided by the glue

Fig. 1-18. An 11-ounce cartridge of drywall construction adhesive designed to fit a standard caulking gun.

Selector Guide for Gypsum Board Nails[1]

fastener description[2]	fastener length (in)	(mm)	total thickness of surfacing materials[3] 1/4 / 6.4	3/8 / 9.5	1/2 / 12.7	5/8 / 15.9	3/4 / 19.1	7/8 / 22.2	1 / 25.4	1-1/4 / 31.8	1-3/8 / 34.9	approx. usage lb/1,000 ft²	kg/100m²
Annular Ring Drywall Nail 12½ ga. (2.50 mm) ¼" (6.35 mm) diam. head, med. diamond point 	1¼	31.8	X	X	X							4.50	2.20
	1⅜	34.9				X						5.00	2.44
	1½	38.1					X					5.25	2.56
	1⅝	41.3						X				5.75	2.81
Same as above except ¹⁹⁄₆₄" (7.54 mm) diam. head	1¼	31.8	X	X	X							4.50	2.20
	1⅜	34.9				X						5.00	2.44
	1½	38.1					X					5.25	2.56
	1⅝	41.3						X				5.75	2.81
	1¾	44.5							X			6.00	2.93
	2	50.8								X		7.00	3.42
12½ ga. (2.50 mm) ¹⁹⁄₆₄" (7.54 mm) diam. head 	1¼	31.8	X	X	X							4.50	2.20
	1⅜	34.9				X						5.00	2.44
	1½	38.1					X					5.25	2.56
	1⅝	41.3						X				5.75	2.81

Selector Guide for Gypsum Board Nails[1] continued

fastener description[2]	fastener length (in)	(mm)	total thickness of surfacing materials[3] 1/4 / 6.4	3/8 / 9.5	1/2 / 12.7	5/8 / 15.9	3/4 / 19.1	7/8 / 22.2	1 / 25.4	1-1/4 / 31.8	1-3/8 / 34.9	approx. usage lb/1,000 ft²	kg/100m²
Same as above except ¼" (6.35 mm) diam. head 14 ga. (2.03 mm)	1⅜ (4d)	34.9				X						3.50	1.71
13½ ga. (2.18 mm)	1⅝ (5d)	41.3					X					4.50	2.20
13 ga. (2.32 mm)	1⅞ (6d)	47.6							X			5.75	2.81
13½ ga. (2.18 mm)	2⅛ (7d)	54.0									X	7.50	3.66
Color Nails for TEXTONE Vinyl Panels 15½ ga. (1.71 mm) ³⁄₃₂" (2.36 mm) diam. head	1⅜	34.9			X	X						2.00	0.98

(1) For wood framing 16" o.c., nails 8" o.c. for walls, 7" o.c. for ceilings.
(2) All nails treated to prevent rust with joint compounds or veneer finishes. Fire-rated assemblies generally require greater nail penetration; therefore, for fire-rated assemblies, use exact nail length and diameter specified for rated assembly (see Fire Test Report).
(3) In laminated double-layer construction, base layer is attached in same manner as single layer.

almost eliminates the chance for joint cracking and nail popping. This is crucial on ceilings. Flaws in ceilings tend to show much worse than on walls. Also, fewer nails are required when glue is used.

The best type of glue to use is called drywall and construction adhesive. It comes in 11-ounce and 29-ounce cartridges for use in a caulking gun, as shown in Fig. 1-18. This type of glue is easily applied and cures quickly. It really holds once it sets up and will fasten most any two building materials.

Chapter 2

Drywalling Tools

With the wide variety of drywalling tools available today, drywall construction is much easier than it once was. Most of the tools discussed in this chapter are designed to take a lot of the work out of drywalling. You should be able to purchase these tools at any good hardware store or building supply.

CUTTING TOOLS

The basic tool used to cut gypsum wallboard is the utility knife (often called a Sheetrock knife). Figure 2-1 illustrates a typical utility knife. The knife has a retractable blade. This is an important safety feature because the blade is extremely sharp. Extra blades can be stored in the handle of the knife.

The utility knife is used to score the paper jacket of the wallboard. The wallboard is then snapped along the cut.

For making curved cuts in gypsum wallboards, any one of several tools can be used. The device shown in Fig. 2-2 is called a circle cutter. It is used like a compass to score the face paper on each side of a gypsum wallboard. The center of the circle is then knocked out with a hammer, leaving a very clean, round hole. The circle cutter is ruled in inches along the arm to indicate the radius of cut. The circle cutter works well for cutting holes for round fixtures such as electrical boxes.

For cutting square holes or making curved cuts in gypsum wallboard, a saw is most handy. A keyhole saw, like the ones shown in Figs. 2-3 and 2-4, is both inexpensive and easy to use. The pointed blade can easily be punched through wallboard to start the cut. The only drawback to using a keyhole saw is that it cuts a bit raggedly. For a cleaner cut, a handheld electric jigsaw like the ones shown in Figs. 2-5 and 2-6 is the best tool to use. Both work equally well.

Many drywallers use a drywall saw (Fig. 2-7) for making some cuts in gypsum wallboard. The blade of this type of saw is very stiff. The teeth of the blade are spaced at about 5 teeth per inch, depending on the manufacturer's preference. The drywall saw is designed for making straight cuts and is most handy for making compound cuts, such as

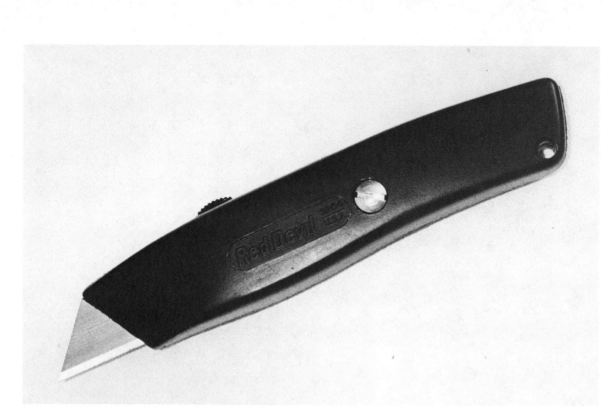

Fig. 2-1. A typical utility knife. Note the button on the back of the handle for retracting the blade. The handle opens by removing the screw, allowing extra blades to be stored inside.

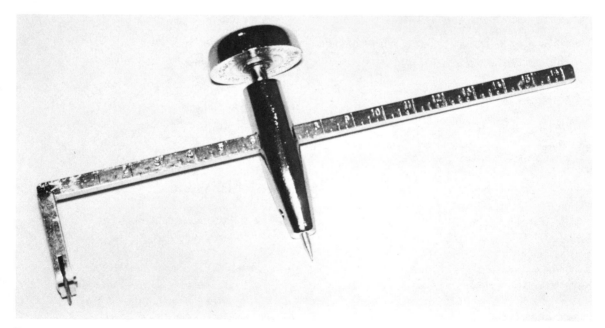

Fig. 2-2. A typical circle cutter. The radius of cut is set by adjusting the center pin on the arm, which is ruled in inches.

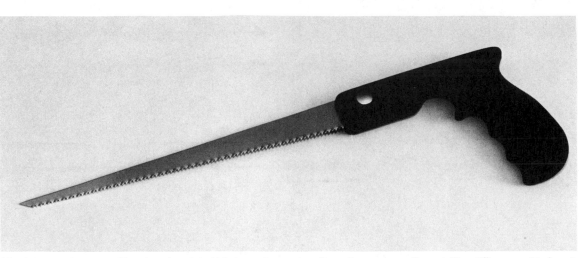

Fig. 2-3. A keyhole saw. The sharply pointed blade easily punches through gypsum wallboard. The stiff, narrow blade cuts curves effectively.

cutting out a corner or a notch from a wallboard.

When cutting gypsum wallboard with a utility knife, a straightedge to guide the knife must be used. A 4-foot T square (Fig. 2-8) is the best straightedge available. It is ruled in inches along the body in opposite directions, allowing you to measure and cut from either end. The T square is a very handy tool. It is useful for many projects, other than drywalling, such as marking plywood sheets or cutting carpet and linoleum.

JOINT FINISHING TOOLS

To properly finish drywall joints, you will need a set of joint-taping and finishing knives. A 6-inch taping knife (Fig. 2-9) is a must. The 6-inch knife is used for filling in nailheads, applying filler coats to all joints, and for embedding paper joint tape in the joints.

A wide-joint finishing knife is used for finishing the intermediate and finish coats of joint compound on the joints. The knife shown in Fig. 2-10 has a 12-inch blade. Blade widths of 8 to 24 inches are available, but 12 inches is by far the most popular width. Different handle lengths are also available (also up to 24 inches in length). As a rule, the shorter the handle the easier the tool will be to use. This is especially true for a beginner. Some joint knives have blades made of fiberglass, but most are made of flexible steel. I prefer a steel blade with a blue coating that prevents rust (Fig. 2-10).

An alternative to the wide-joint knife is a curved-joint trowel (Fig. 2-11). This type of joint trowel is particularly handy for finishing the butt joints created at the ends of the wallboards where no valley is present. The curve of the blade makes a crown that allows you to hide the joint tape easily.

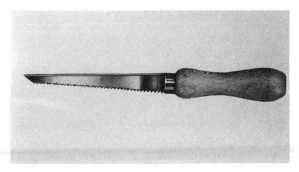

Fig. 2-4. A drywall utility saw is very similar to the keyhole saw (courtesy of Goldblatt Tool Company).

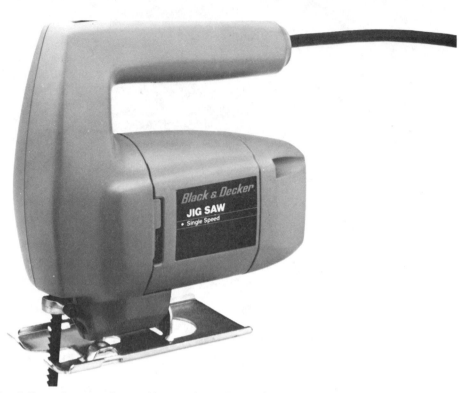

Fig. 2-5. A single-speed electric jigsaw is an excellent and inexpensive tool to use for cutting gypsum wallboard (courtesy of Black & Decker (U.S.) Inc.).

Fig. 2-6. A variable-speed electric reciprocating saw similar to a jigsaw (courtesy of Black & Decker (U.S.) Inc.).

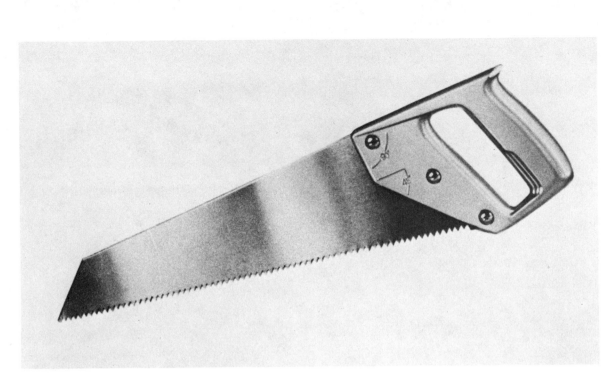

Fig. 2-7. A drywall saw (courtesy of Goldlbatt Tool Company).

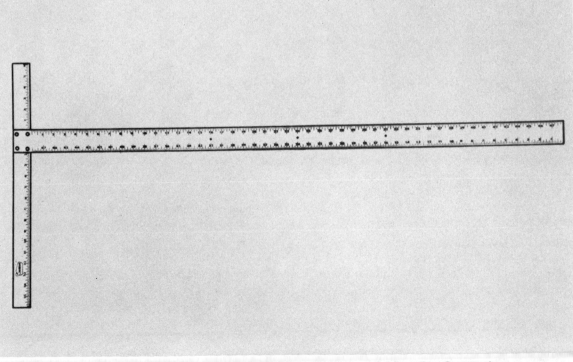

Fig. 2-8. A typical drywalling T square is an extremely useful tool (courtesy of Goldblatt Tool Company).

Fig. 2-9. A 6-inch joint taping knife used for applying filler coats of joint compound to the drywall joints and nailheads.

Curved joint trowels are available in blade lengths of 10, 12, or 14 inches (again 12 inches is the most popular width). The curved-joint trowel also works well on valley joints. I own both a 12-inch joint knife and a 12-inch curved joint trowel. I use the joint knife for finishing valley joints and the curved trowel for finishing butt joints.

One very handy tool to have is a corner-finishing trowel. A typical corner trowel is shown in Fig. 2-12. The corner trowel is used to apply joint compound and joint tape to inside corner joints. It takes a great deal of the work out of finishing the inside corners and lets you produce professional results with ease. Even if you only use it once, this tool is a good investment.

Along with a set of joint knives, you will also need a tray or pan to scoop the joint compound from as you are applying it. The best item to use for this is a mud pan (Fig. 2-13). It is 12 inches long and

roughly 4 inches wide. You can purchase mud pans made of plastic or steel in lengths of 12 to 24 inches. As you might have guessed, 12-inch mud pans are the most popular. The pan shown in Fig. 2-13 is made of plastic and has removable steel edges. The steel edges are handy for scraping the blade of your joint knives clean, something you must do often when applying joint compound.

Once the joint compound on the joint has dried, it must be sanded smooth. There are several tools available for making this task go quickly and easily. One such tool is a pole sander (Fig. 2-14). The pole sander is basically a sanding pad attached to a broom handle by a universal joint. The sandpaper is held over a rubber cushion by clamps that easily tighten with wing nuts. The sanding head unscrews from the handle. This allows 2-foot handle extensions to be added or the sanding head to be changed. The tool shown in Fig. 2-14 holds half a sheet of

Fig. 2-10. A 12-inch joint finishing knife used for applying second and finish coats of joint compound to drywall joints. The blade is made of flexible steel and is coated with a rust inhibitor.

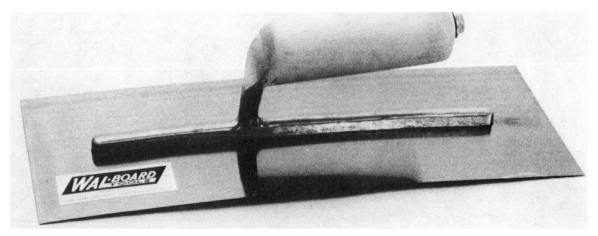

Fig. 2-11. A 12-inch curved joint finishing trowel. The curvature of the blade makes the tool very effective for finishing butt joints in drywall systems with the proper crown (courtesy of Wallboard Tool Company).

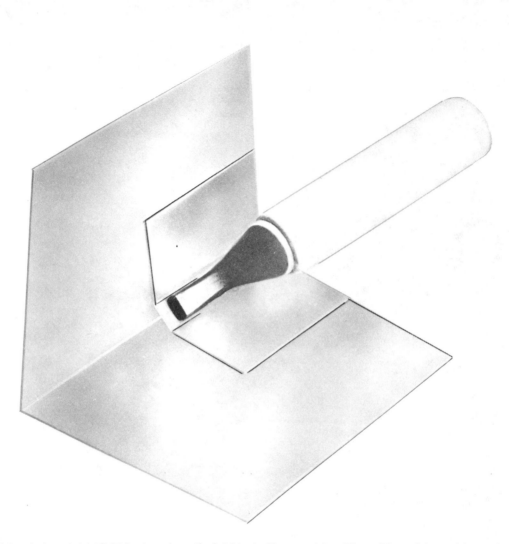

Fig. 2-12. A typical corner joint finishing trowel used for finishing inside corner joints. The tool does all the work for you (courtesy of Red Devil Inc.).

8-×-12-inch sandpaper.

The tool in Fig. 2-15 is an angle sander. It is similar to the pole sander, except that it is used for sanding inside corner joints. The sanding head is hinged in the center. A spring applies continuous tension between the sanding planes, so that pressure is applied to both sides of the corner joint during sanding. The angle sander holds a half sheet of 8-×-12-inch sandpaper.

The best type of sandpaper to use for sanding drywall joints is an open-coat sandpaper at either #100 or #120 grit. It is rough enough to take down the dried joint compound rapidly, yet smooth enough so the face paper on the wallboards is not too easily roughened.

Precut pieces of sandpaper that fit the sanding heads previously discussed are available. I usually buy #100-grit sheets at 8 by 12 inches and fold them in half. When the first side wears out, I flip them over.

Sanding drywall joints is a messy task that generates a great deal of dust. It is wise to wear a

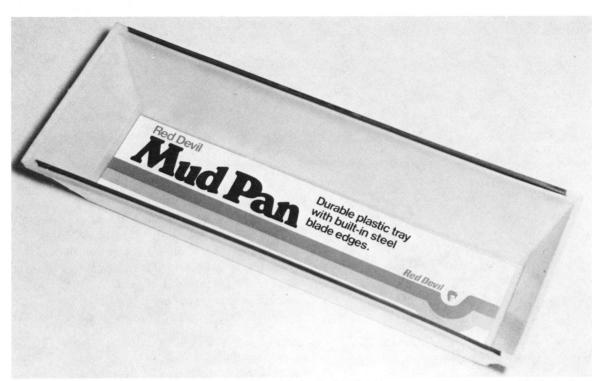

Fig. 2-13. A typical mud pan used to apply joint compound during the joint finishing process. Note the removable steel edges used to scrape joint knives clean.

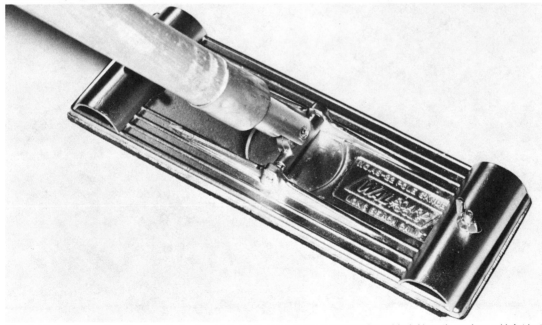

Fig. 2-14. A pole sander. The handle is about 5 feet long and extensions may be added. Note the universal joint between the handle and the head.

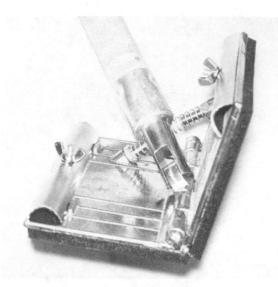

Fig. 2-15. An angle sander used for sanding inside corner joints. The spring between the sanding planes maintains pressure on the sides of the joint during sanding.

dust mask during sanding. Modern joint compounds no longer contain asbestos, but breathing the dust is still not advisable. Two types of dust mask are available. The one shown in Fig. 2-16 has removable, washable filters and offers excellent protection against floating particles of dust or paint. The dust mask shown in Fig. 2-17 is disposable and protects equally well. I prefer the disposable paper masks because they are slightly more comfortable to wear and don't seem to make me sweat as much.

OTHER USEFUL TOOLS

There are a few other tools that make drywalling faster, easier, and more pleasurable. Some are necessities, while others are conveniences. One such tool is a drywalling hammer (Fig. 2-18). The face of the hammer is rounded to create the proper dimple around the nailhead in the wallboard as the nail is driven "home." The face is also serrated like

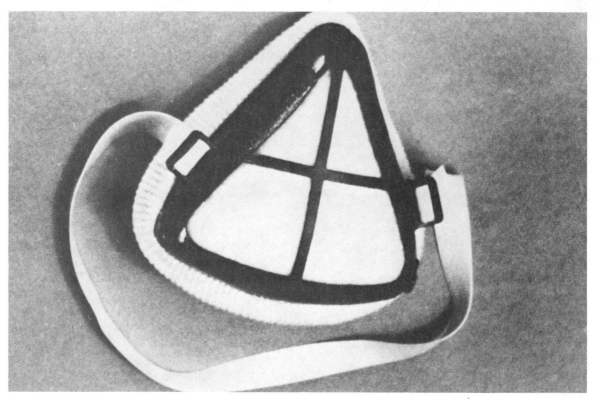

Fig. 2-16. A typical dust mask. The filters may be removed for cleaning or replaced completely (courtesy of Black & Decker (U.S.) Inc.).

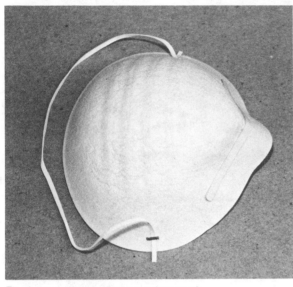

Fig. 2-17. A disposable paper dust mask.

notch in the blade is for pulling nails. Most drywall hammers weigh about 12 ounces; as hammers go they are rather light. The drywall hammer is a very effective tool. If you are short on cash, you can do just as well with a 16-ounce framing hammer. A 20-ounce hammer is a bit heavy for drywalling.

The device shown in Fig. 2-19 is a wallboard roller-lifter. It is used to lift gypsum wallboards from the floor into the proper position against the wall studs for nailing. The lip of the tool slips under the edge of the wallboard. Foot pressure is used to raise the wallboard into place where the proper contact is made between the sheet being lifted and the adjoining sheet. The roller wheel is mounted so that, as the front raises, it also moves forward— keeping the wallboard against the studs. The tool is also weighted to rest lip down so you can kick it along as you work.

A common caulking gun is shown in Fig. 2-20. You will need one to apply glue to the studs and joists prior to nailing up the wallboards. This gun holds a standard 11-ounce cartridge of glue or caulking. Guns large enough to hold a 29-ounce cartridge are also available. You will get more use out of an 11-ounce gun. The 11-ounce cartridge is

a miniature waffle iron to prevent it from slipping off the nailhead during nailing and damaging the wallboard. The blade of the hammer is not intended for cutting. It is dull on the edge and is used for prying or jacking wallboards into position. The

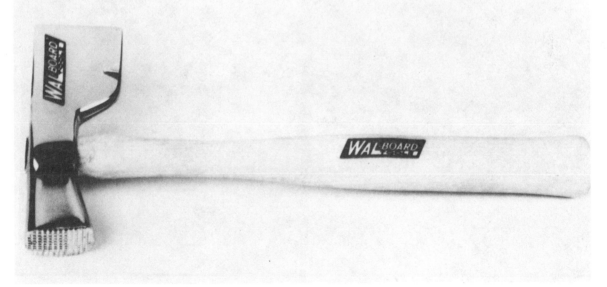

Fig. 2-18. A drywalling hammer. The rounded face creates a dimple in the face of the wallwoard as the nail is driven. The serrations on the face prevent the hammer from slipping off the nail during driving (courtesy of Wallboard Tool Company).

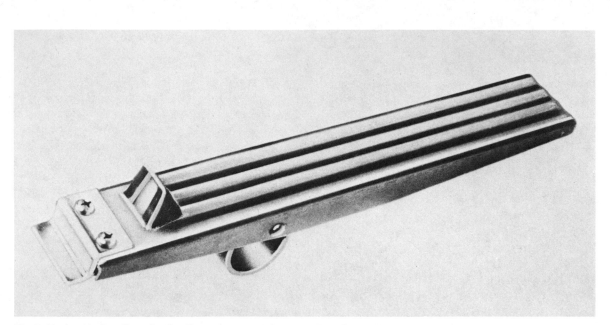

Fig. 2-19. A typical wallboard roller-lifter (courtesy of Goldblatt Tool Company).

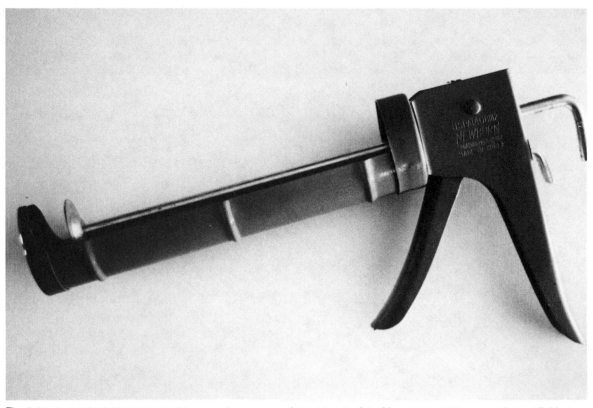

Fig. 2-20. A standard 11-ounce caulking gun. Larger guns that accommodate 29-ounce cartridges are also available.

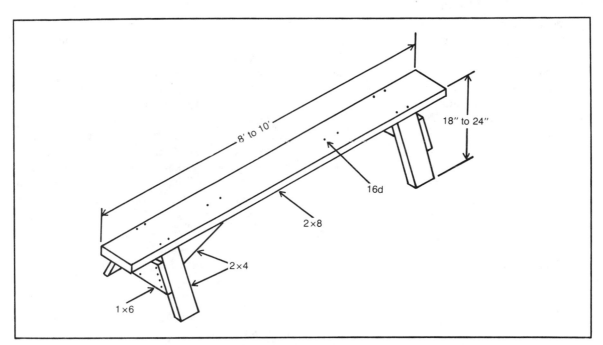

Fig. 2-21. A typical drywalling bench. The dimensions can be changed to suit the requirements of the user.

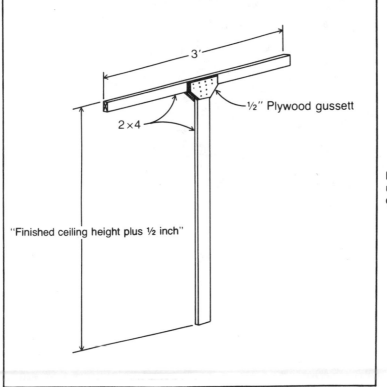

Fig. 2-22. A T brace, also called a shore, used to brace gypsum wallboard against ceiling joists for easier nailing.

the most common size for glue, caulking, glazing compounds, and similar products.

Something you will surely need is a sturdy bench to stand on while you are drywalling the ceiling. Figure 2-21 shows the type of bench I have found most useful. Not only is it a good drywalling bench, but it also makes a good sawhorse. The height of your bench will depend on how tall you are. For drywalling a standard 8-foot ceiling, a bench between 18 and 24 inches should be about right. You will need the bench for hanging the wallboards and finishing the joints on the ceiling. You will be walking on it. When you build it, use both nails and drywall construction adhesive to fasten the parts together.

A pair of T braces (Fig. 2-22) will make your drywall projects go much easier. The T braces (sometimes called shores) are used to hold gypsum wallboards in place against the ceiling joists during nailing. The braces should be about ½ inch taller than your finished ceiling height. Once the wallboard is positioned on the ceiling joists, the braces are wedged between the floor and the wallboard to hold it, freeing both hands for nailing.

If you are modifying or adding to an existing drywall system, you will have to locate studs or joists in the walls and ceiling. You can "tap them out" by pounding on the walls or you can use a studfinder like one of those in Figs. 2-23 and 2-24. The studfinder shown in Fig. 2-23 magnetically finds the nailheads embedded in the gypsum wallboards, indicating the presence of a framing member. The

Fig. 2-23. A typical magnetic studfinder. The encased needle will point to a nailhead as a compass needle points north.

Fig. 2-24. An electronic studfinder. The indicators on the front light from bottom to top as you approach a stud or joist (courtesy of Zircon International Inc.).

device shown in Fig. 2-24 is called a stud sensor. It electronically locates studs and joists by measuring changes in density in the wall or ceiling. As you approach a framing member, the indictors on the face of the instrument light from the bottom to the top. I own a stud sensor exactly like the one shown in Fig. 2-24, and I have found it extremely useful for every project from hanging pictures to adding rooms. It is impeccably accurate and easy to use.

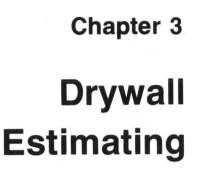

Chapter 3

Drywall Estimating

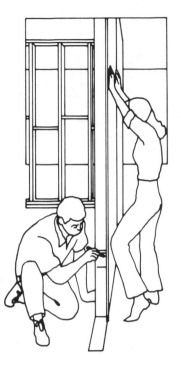

Before you can hang the first sheet or drive the first nail, you must take a moment to estimate the amounts of time and material required to complete your project. A simple "guestimate" won't do. The typical beginner will most often look over the area he plans to improve and think something like, "I can knock this out for just a few bucks over a weekend!" Then, as he is leaving the lumberyard, he is amazed at the money he has spent. Worse yet, he ends up making several trips back for the material he didn't get enough of the first time. A good estimate simply makes life much easier, and your project more enjoyable to do.

YOUR TIME

Estimating how much time it will take to complete your project will take a little guess work on your part. It depends on how handy you are, whether or not you are working alone, and the extent of the job you are facing.

Even if you are pretty handy, allow three full days for even the smallest drywalling project. This is assuming that you hang all the gypsum panels and tape all of the joints in the first day. It also assumes that you finish the joints with no more than three coats of joint compound, allowing a full 24 hours between each coat for drying time.

Using a typical 10-by-12-foot room as an example, five to seven days is a more reasonable guess.

GYPSUM WALLBOARD REQUIREMENTS

The first step in figuring how many wallboards you will need is determining what size sheet you will use. Table 3-1 shows the various requirements and conditions you must consider when fastening gypsum wallboard to the interior walls of a structure. Table 3-1 is based on the requirements from the *One & Two Family Dwelling Code*. This code is a widely recognized standard that specifies in great detail the minimum structural requirements of residential construction. You can read more about it in Chapter 9. Table 3-1 will help you select the proper sheet thickness, nail size, and nail spacing.

Table 3-1. Drywall Fastening Requirements Based on the Specifications of Various Building Codes.

Without Glue					
Sheet Thickness	Nailing Surface	Sheet Direction	Framing Member Spacing	Nail Spacing	Nail Size and Type
$\frac{1}{2}$ "	Ceiling	Either	16"	Double	1⅜ or 5D ring shank or cement coated sinker
	Ceiling	Across	24"	7	
	Wall	Either	24"	8"	
$\frac{5}{8}$ "	Ceiling	Either	16"	7"	1⅝" or 6D ring shank or cement coated sinker
	Ceiling	Across	24"	7"	
	Wall	Either	24"	Double	
With Glue					
$\frac{1}{2}$ or $\frac{5}{8}$ "	Ceiling	Either	16"	16"	Same as without glue
	Ceiling	Across	24"	12"	
	Wall	Either	24"	24"	
$\frac{3}{8}$ " double ply	Ceiling	Across	24"	16"	Base same as ½" face glue only
	Wall	Either	24"	24"	
Double nails are pairs of nails 2 to 2½ inches apart Between nails and no more than 12 inches between each pair of nails.					

Two things should be considered in selecting sheet length. One is the price per sheet. A 12-foot sheet normally costs almost twice as much as an 8-foot sheet.

The second factor is the number of joints and their length that will occur between sheets. You will have far fewer joints to finish if you use 12-foot sheets. I feel this is the most important of the two. When I work up an estimate, this is the deciding factor. Joint finishing is the messiest, sweatiest part of the job. Reducing this task to a minimum should be your primary goal throughout the entire project.

Try to use 12-foot sheets wherever you can. If you intend to cover a wall or ceiling that is more than 8 feet, but 12 feet or less in length, use 12-foot sheets. If the wall or ceiling is greater than 12 feet, but 20 feet or less in length, you can mix 8-foot and 12-foot sheets for the greatest economy with the least amount of joints.

Suppose you have a ceiling or wall that is 16 feet long. Would you choose to cover it with two courses of 8-foot sheets? Probably so, but you shouldn't. The best method would be to cover it with 12-foot sheets and 8-footers cut in half. This would allow you to offset the butt joints at the ends of the sheets 4 feet apart. The benefits of staggering the joints in this manner are discussed at length in Chapters 4 and 5.

The best method for covering walls is to use 12-foot sheets hung horizontally. Placing the sheets horizontally produces a single valley joint around the room 4 feet high. This is a very easy joint to finish. The use of 12-foot sheets again produces fewer butt joints at the ends of the sheets. As with the ceiling, you can mix 12-foot and 8-foot sheets to save money.

Estimate the number of each size sheet you need first for the ceiling, and then for each wall individually. This will give you the opportunity to carefully think of how you will place each sheet on the framing members. It will also help to keep you from spending more money than you need to. In fact, it is not a bad idea to make a scale diagram of each wall and ceiling you are covering. Figure 3-1 shows a diagram of two methods for covering the same wall. The wall is 8 feet tall, as are most walls, and 14 feet long. It has a window opening that is 2½ by 3½ feet.

Plan A uses 8-foot sheets coursed vertically. It requires 4 sheets. Plan B uses two 12-foot sheets and one 8-foot sheet coursed horizontally. Let's compare the two plans.

In comparing plan A and plan B, first consider cost. Assume that an 8-foot sheet costs $3.50. Assume also that a 12-foot sheet costs $6.25. These are realistic assumptions at the time of this printing. If my slide rule is correct, the cost of plan A would be $14.00. The cost of plan B would be $16.00.

Now let's look at the amount of joints that each plan produces. Plan A creates 24 feet of joint, all running vertically. Plan B creates only 19½ feet, most of which runs horizontally. Remember, you have to finish these joints later. The joints in plan B are much easier to finish, and the cuts are easier to make too. The waste factor for both plans is exactly the same, half an 8-foot sheet.

In light of all this, plan B is the best way to go. The extra $2 is well spent in regard to saving time and sweat. I would choose plan B, hands down.

When you are preparing your estimate, do not subtract the area of the door and window openings in the walls. These seem to provide a "built-in" waste factor. Figure your walls as though they were solid, with no openings at all. The only exceptions might be a garage door or an extremely large picture window.

FASTENER REQUIREMENTS

Refer once again to Table 3-1. As I said earlier in this chapter, the table specifies nail size and nail spacing requirements for gypsum wallboard attachment. Note that fewer nails are required when the panels are nailed and glued to the studs or joists. This should convince you to use glue.

Once again using the 10-by-12-foot room as an example, plan to use at least 3 pounds of nails. You should get about 300 drywall nails to the pound. The 3-pound figure is just a minimum. You might very well use more, depending on stud or joist spacing, the length of the wallboards, and the number and size of the openings in the walls. Nails are inexpensive. It is not a bad idea to pick up an extra pound or two. It might save you an extra trip to the lumberyard.

JOINT REINFORCEMENT REQUIREMENTS

When you determine the size and the number of wallboards you will need, you also have a good idea of how many feet of joint you will have to finish. Simply purchase enough paper joint tape to cover it. For that 10-by-12-foot room, a 100-foot roll will usually do.

Purchase enough metal corner bead to cover the outside corners that occur in the rooms and at the doorways. If the doorway will have a door installed in it, there is no need to bead the corners. This is also true if you intend to trim it with wooden molding.

Don't try to save a few pennies by piecing together the parts you cut from full lengths. Corner beads come in 8-foot lengths. Most doors are 6 feet 8 inches tall. Allow five beads for each doorway (it's acceptable to cut the top one in half and use both pieces).

JOINT COMPOUND REQUIREMENTS

It's hard to say how much mud a beginner is liable to use. In fact, it might be a guess at best. For that average-size room we have been using as an example throughout this chapter, buy one 5-gallon bucket of joint compound. You will use most, if not all, of it for the first two coats. You might have enough left for the final coat. If you don't, you can buy a smaller 1 or 2-gallon pail and save a few dollars. The final coat is extremely thin and won't require as much mud as the first two. This, of course, assumes you

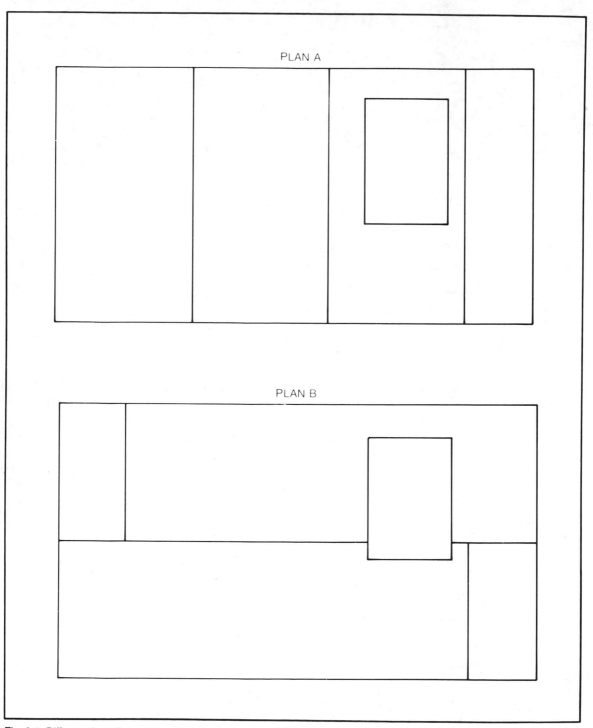

PLAN A

PLAN B

Fig. 3-1. Different drywall coverage plans for the same wall. Plan A produces 24 feet of joint. Plan B produces only 19½. The long horizontal joint in plan B will be much easier to finish than the vertical joints in plan A.

Nails	
Nail size	Lbs/1000 sq. ft.
1¼"	4½"
1⅜"	5
1½"	5¼
1⅝"	5¾
1¾"	6
1⅞	6½
2"	7
2⅛"	7½
Pre-mixed joint compound	
140 lbs (12 gallons) per 1000 square feet of wallboard	
Paper joint tape	
375 linear feet per 100 square feet of wallboard	
Drywall construction adhesive	
3 gallons (18 11-ounce cartridges) per 1000 square feet of wallboard	

Table 3-2. Drywall Estimating Guide.

Table 3-3. Wallboard Estimating Guide.

Gypsum Wallboards		
Wallboard size (feet)	Wallboard area (square feet)	Wallboards /1000 sq. ft.
4×8	32	32
4×9	36	28
4×10	40	25
4×12	48	21
4×14	56	18
4×16	64	16

can produce satisfactory results in three coats.

It is always wise to add in a small waste factor. For example, say you require 15 gypsum wallboards. Recall from Chapter 1 that wallboards come packaged in pairs. It is inexpensive insurance to take the other sheet and get 16 instead.

LARGE DRYWALLING PROJECTS

Tables 3-2 and 3-3 are drywall materials estimating guides. They give quantities of wallboards, nails, glue, joint tape, and joint compound required per thousand square feet of wallboard coverage.

The amounts in the tables will vary some based on factors previously discussed, but—for the most part—they are pretty close and already have the waste factor figured in. Therefore, a 1000-square-foot room would measure approximately 19 × 20 feet.

Chapter 4
Gypsum Wallboard Application

Fastening gypsum wallboards to the framing, or drywall "hanging," is a simple process. There are a few tricks that make it much easier and enhance the appearance of the finished job. By paying close attention to a few details, you will be able to produce professional results and even have some fun doing it.

BEFORE YOU START

There are a few things you should check before you start hanging drywall on the walls and ceiling. At this point, I must assume that you have some basic knowledge of how a house is built or at least how a wall or ceiling is framed. Illustrations of acceptable framing practices can be found in Appendix A.

Make sure that the edges of all the wall studs and ceiling joists are flush. The best method of doing this is to run a string along the edges as shown in Fig. 4-1. Simply sighting along the edges with your eye won't do. Knock out and replace any stud that is bowed or crooked. Being ⅛ of an inch off on a stud is no cause for alarm, but one that runs out

more than ¼ of an inch should be replaced.

Be sure there is an adequate nailing surface to attach the wallboards to at all the wall and ceiling corners. Figure 4-2 shows a nailer that has been "scabbed" to the top of the wall plates for the corner of the ceiling sheet. Also check the spacing of the studs and joists. The edge of each wallboard must fall half onto a framing member. Move any stud or joist that is off or scab a nailer to it.

Check all electrical boxes for installation at the proper depth. For example, if you are covering the walls with ½-inch thick wallboards, the front edge of the box should not protrude past the edge of the stud more than ½ inch. It is a good practice to mount all electrical boxes at an ⅛ inch less than the wallboard thickness being hung. This is shown in Fig. 4-3. As shown in Fig. 4-3, ½-inch wallboard will be used so the box is mounted on the stud at ⅜ inch. This practice is also advisable for other fixtures such as heating and air-conditioning vents and registers.

Check the holes in the studs and joists where

Fig. 4-1. Using a string to check the straightness of wall studs.

Fig. 4-2. A nailer has been scabbed to the wall plates to provide a nailing surface for the corner of the wallboard on the ceiling.

Building permits and inspections are covered in detail in Chapter 9.

NAILING GYPSUM WALLBOARD

You are probably somewhat proficient at driving nails already. Nailing gypsum wallboard is a little different from nailing wood, however, so I will provide a few pointers here.

A nail apron and a hammer loop are absolute necessities. Without them, a three-day project can easily turn into a three-week nightmare. The same can be said about a helper. You can probably cover the walls by yourself, but the ceiling can be pretty tough to do alone. This is especially true if you are using 12-foot wallboards. You might think you can do the ceilings alone by using T braces. If you are brave enough to attempt this, buy a hard hat first. Hoisting a 60- or 90-pound wallboard over your head "just long enough" to wedge a T brace under it can be a very frustrating task.

The drywall nails need not be driven exactly perpendicular to the face of the wallboard. In fact, a slight angle of drive will increase the holding power of the nail. When you swing a hammer, your arm does not travel in a straight line. It makes an arc. Place each nail so that, as your arm completes its natural swing, the face of the hammer meets the nailhead squarely. Doing this will ensure straight, clean drives with few bent or missed nails. In addition, your arm will tire less rapidly, especially when you're nailing on the ceiling.

Don't try to thunder the nails in with two or three swats. That's acceptable for rough framing, but with drywalling you can't afford to miss or bend nails and smash up the wallboards.

When you drive each nail "home," dimple the surface of the wallboard slightly; take care not to break the face paper or crush the gypsum core of the wallboard. The dimpling is done so that the nailhead can be buried under joint compound during the joint finishing process. A properly dimpled nailhead is shown in Fig. 4-6.

Always double-nail wherever possible. Instead of placing one nail every 8 inches, place pairs of nails at 12-inch intervals. The individual nails of

electrical wires pass through. They should be centered like the one shown in Fig. 4-4. If the hole was too close to either edge of the stud, a nail might easily be driven through the wire, creating a short circuit that would be almost impossible to find.

Mark the position of each stud on the subfloor as shown in Fig. 4-5. This will enable you to quickly and easily find each stud when the time comes to attach the baseboard molding to the walls.

If you were required to purchase a building permit prior to beginning your project, be absolutely certain that you have passed all the required plumbing, mechanical, and electrical rough-in inspections before you cover up the walls and ceiling.

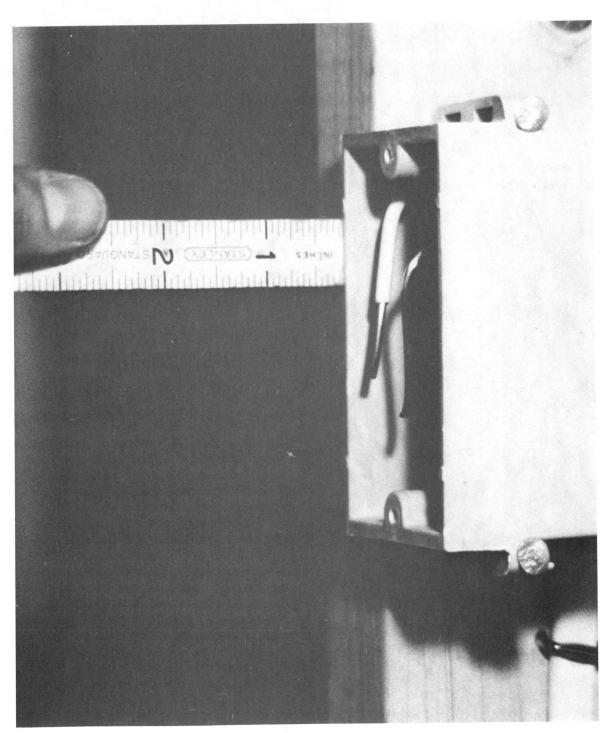

Fig. 4-3. Checking the depth of an electrical box on a stud.

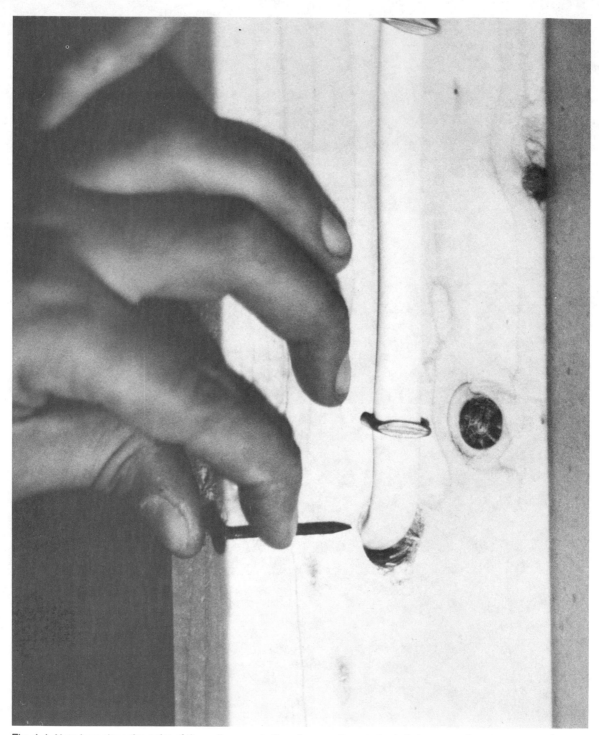

Fig. 4-4. Note how close the point of the nail comes to the wire even though the hole is centered on the stud. The nail is a 1¼-incher, the shortest drywall nail available.

Fig. 4-5. Marking the location of a stud on the subfloor.

Fig. 4-6. Close-up of a properly dimpled nailhead. Note that the gypsum core of the wallboard is not damaged and the face paper is not torn.

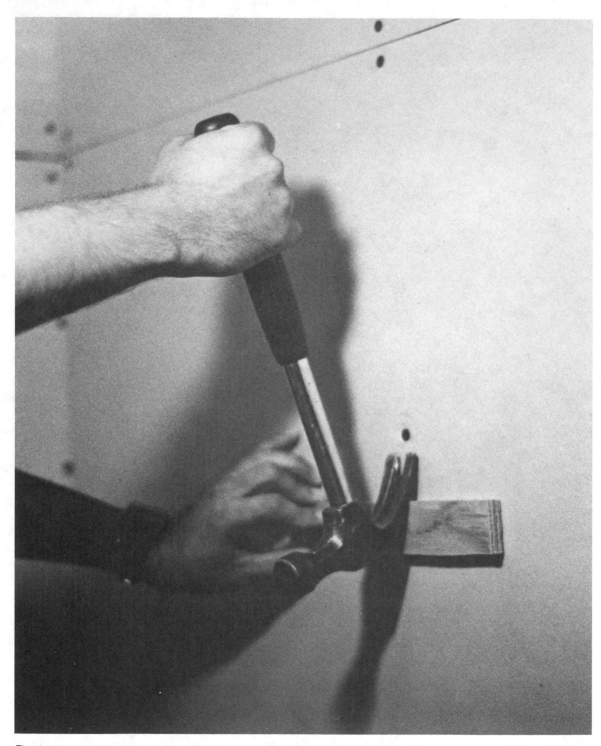

Fig. 4-7. Using a shim to protect the face of a gypsum wallboard while pulling a nail.

each pair should be 2 inches but no more than 2½ inches apart.

In the event you must pull a nail out (even I bent one once), insert a shim under the head of the hammer as shown in Fig. 4-7. This will prevent you from scarring the face of the wallboard. When you drive the new nail, do not try to use the same hole. Move about 2 inches away from where you pulled the first nail.

CUTTING GYPSUM WALLBOARD

Cutting gypsum wallboard is a simple process when done properly. Actually, it's kind of fun. It's literally a "snap" as you will find as you read on. When cutting gypsum wallboard, as with anything else, it is always a good practice to measure twice and cut once. If you cut a piece too short, no matter how many more times you cut it, it will still be too short.

Making straight cuts in wallboard is basically a three-step process. First, lay the wallboard flat with the finish side up. All cuts are made from the finish side first. Very carefully measure and mark the wallboard with a T square. Without moving the square, make the initial cut by drawing the blade of your utility knife along the edge of the square, cutting through the face paper and into the wallboard about 1/16 inch as shown in Fig. 4-8. Keep the hand that holds the square well away from the knife. A utility knife that has a fresh blade in it can slice off a fingertip in a fraction of a second.

Next, stand the wallboard up on edge. Snap it at the cut from the back side. Hold it with both hands and give it a little kick with your knee as shown in Fig. 4-9. Once you have snapped it, bend the sides of the wallboard back until they form a right angle. Take care not to pull the paper away from the back of the panels as you fold them.

The final step is to cut the backing paper with the utility knife. Start the cut from the bottom of the

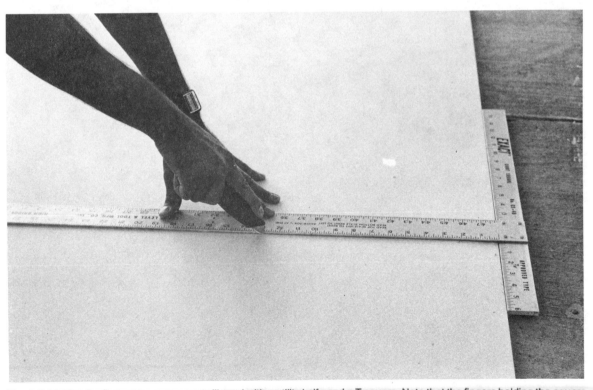

Fig. 4-8. Making the first cut in a gypsum wallboard with a utility knife and a T square. Note that the fingers holding the square are well away from the edge of the square.

Fig. 4-9. Snapping a gypsum wallboard after making the first cut.

sheet. The angle formed by the fold will help you guide the blade (Fig. 4-10). The result should be a straight, clean edge. If the edge is a little ragged, use the utility knife to trim it off smooth. This is the basic method of cutting gypsum wallboard.

Compound cuts that change direction or make angles can be done with a drywall saw. They can also be cut with a utility knife and a T square using the following method.

Carefully measure (twice) and mark the wallboard as in Fig. 4-11. Hold the square firmly during marking. Next, using a nail or an awl, punch a hole completely through the wallboard at each corner of the cut. In Fig. 4-12, a 16-penny nail is being used to punch the holes.

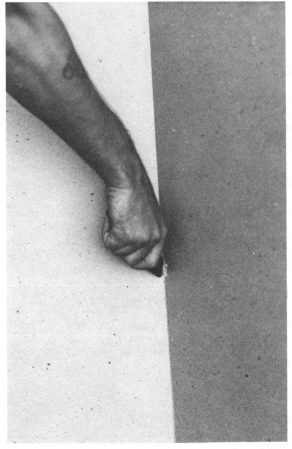

Fig. 4-10. Making the final cut in a gypsum wallboard. The folded edges of the wallboard are used as a guide for the knife blade.

Once the holes are punched, cut the finish side of the wallboard with the utility knife and the square as was explained for making straight cuts. Then, very carefully, flip the wallboard over onto the other side. Cut the backing paper between the holes, duplicating the first cut. You could mark the back side prior to cutting it if you like, but the holes should provide a reliable guide for the square.

The final step is to carefully, very carefully, stand the wallboard on edge. Then simply snap the cuts with a little kick of your knee. You should get a nice crisp cut like the one shown in Fig. 4-13.

Cutting holes in gypsum wallboards can be done in several ways. For cutting round holes, either a saw or a circle cutter should be used. The circle cutter is used much like a compass to score through the paper of the wallboard is shown in Fig. 4-14. Score both sides of the wallboard for the best results. Once that is done, knock the center out of the hole with a hammer. It should pop out in one piece like the one shown in Fig. 4-15, leaving a very clean, round circle. If it's a bit rough, trim it out with a utility knife.

Cutting square holes like those required for electrical boxes is best done with a saw. After carefully measuring and marking the hole, the cut is made from the finish side of the wallboard. It is a good idea to make the hole a bit larger than required. This ensures easy fitting of the wallboard over the box. Figure 4-16 shows a keyhole saw is being used to make the cut. The blade is punched through the wallboard to start the cut. When cutting wallboards with a keyhole saw, go slowly and pay close attention to the travel of the blade. Use short strokes. This way the edge of the cut won't be too ragged, and the paper won't be ripped away from the gypsum core.

Figure 4-17 shows an electric jigsaw being used to cut a hole. The jigsaw produces an extremely smooth edge. Gypsum wallboard offers little resistance to the jigsaw. Take care not to let the saw run away from you. Hold the saw firmly against the wallboard, but not so firmly that you scar the face paper of the panel.

Square holes can also be cut with a utility knife. Once the hole is marked, punch holes at each corner

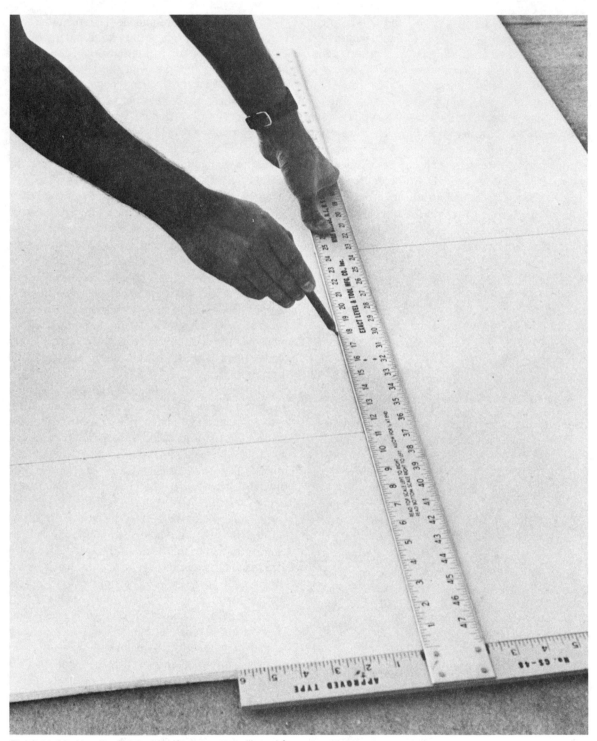

Fig. 4-11. Marking the finish side of a gypsum wallboard for a compound cut.

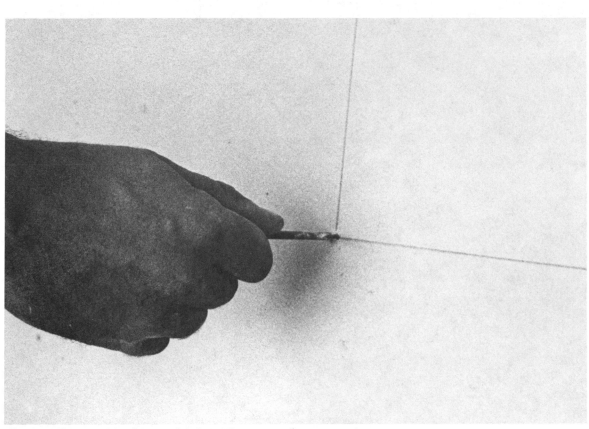

Fig. 4-12. Using a 16d nail to punch holes at the corners of a compound cut.

of the cut to be made. Cut between the holes with the utility knife on both sides of the wallboard, and then knock the center out with a hammer. This is just like the compound-cut method previously explained.

DRYWALLING THE CEILING

Always start a drywalling project by covering the ceiling first. There are several reasons for doing this. The wallboards on the walls must support the edges of those on the ceilings. Therefore, it follows that the ones on the ceiling must go up first. Also, there are far fewer rough openings in most ceilings. This will postpone the need to chop up your wallboards for a while. Also, because the ceiling is the toughest part to cover, you get the worst part over with first.

At this point you have decided in which direc-

tion to run the long dimension of the wallboards. Wherever practical, it is best to place the length of the sheet perpendicular to the ceiling joists. Doing so provides increased structural stability in the drywall system and reduces the chance of joint cracks or nail pops occurring. The deciding factor, however, should be the amount and type of joints created and the ease of finishing those joints. Procedures for determining these factors are detailed in Chapter 3. Both gluing and double-nailing the wallboards will so significantly reduce the chances of joint cracks and nail pops that sheet direction becomes merely academic.

The wallboards on the ceiling should always be glued and double-nailed in place. The weight of the wallboards on the ceiling pulls directly downward on the nails, increasing the chance of nail pops and joint cracks. This is especially true if there is a floor

Fig. 4-13. Snapping a gypsum wallboard along compound cut lines made with a utility knife and T square.

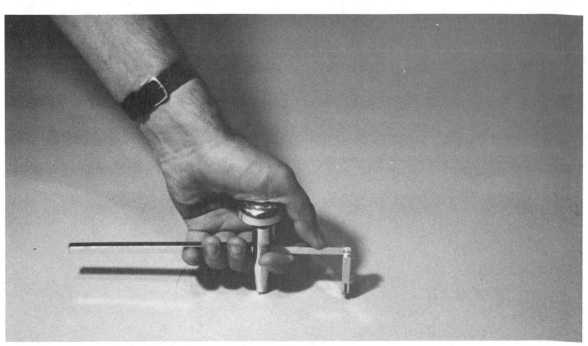

Fig. 4-14. Scoring the finish side of a gypsum wallboard with a circle cutter.

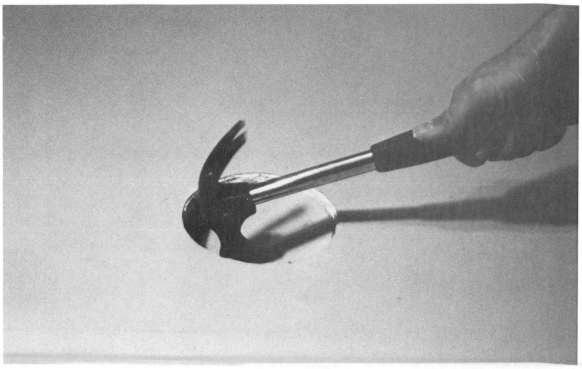

Fig. 4-15. Knocking the center out of a hole made with a circle cutter.

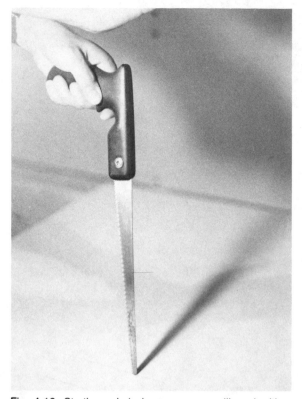

with a live load directly above. Glueing and double-nailing the ceiling wallboards all but eliminates those chances.

Once you select a sheet direction, stick with it. Avoid placing the square end of a wallboard against the tapered edge of another. This will make the joints easier to finish. How easy your joints are to finish might well determine how well they are finished, and directly affect the appearance of the finished job. Flaws in ceiling joints tend to be much more noticeable because of the way light from the ceiling fixtures strikes them.

Begin covering the ceiling in a corner, preferably one where you can start off with a full sheet. As I said earlier, you should be using glue. Chop the tip of the cartridge off at a 45-degree angle at a point where it will extrude a ⅜-inch bead of glue (as in Fig. 4-18). There are two patterns for applying glue to the ceiling joints. These patterns are shown in Fig. 4-19. On the joists that fall in the center of a wallboard, a single bead of glue down the middle of the joist will do. On the joists at the edges of the wallboards, the glue should be applied in the S-pattern illustrated. The S-pattern applys glue to two adjoining wallboards at once. Some drywallers apply two straight beads of glue, one on each edge of

Fig. 4-16. Starting a hole in a gypsum wallboard with a keyhole saw.

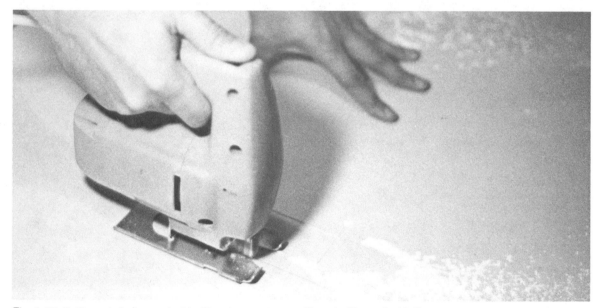

Fig. 4-17. Cutting a hole for an electrical box in a gypsum wallboard with an electric jigsaw.

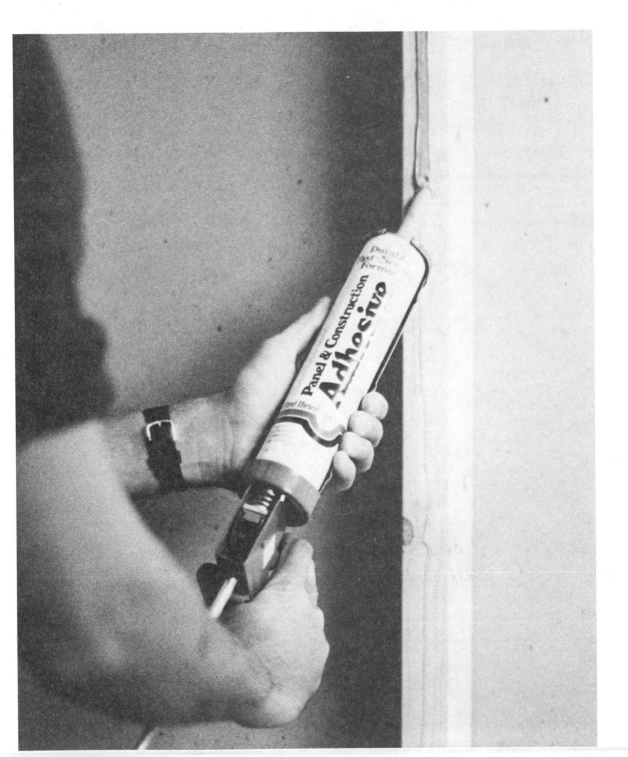

Fig. 4-18. Applying a bead of glue to a wall stud with a caulking gun.

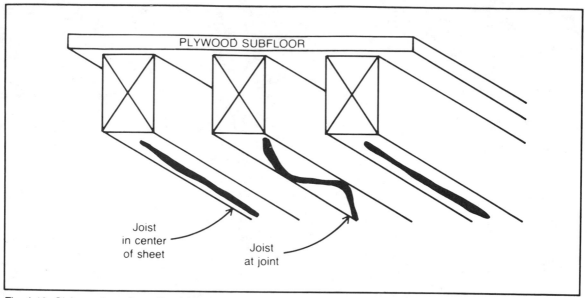

Fig. 4-19. Gluing patterns for ceiling joists.

the joist at the joints. Others don't glue the edges of the wallboards at all. I glue them and so should you. Gypsum wallboards don't crack in the center; they crack at the joints. Gluing the wallboard edges is good insurance against joint cracking.

If it is necessary to install furring strips on the ceiling joists to correct framing problems, use 2 × 2-inch nominal framing lumber. Do not use 1 × 4 or 1 × 2. As you drive nails into 1 × 4 or smaller lumber, the vibration produced causes the nails you have already driven into the furring strip to pop loose. There are also metal furring systems available, but they require you to screw the wallboards to the furring strips.

As you place the wallboards on the ceiling, butt them firmly against the wall plates at the ceiling perimeter. If a wallboard doesn't fit squarely into a corner, trim it to fit. This is necessary so the edges of the sheets on the wall can support the edges of those you are hanging on the ceiling.

When you place adjacent sheets, make only light contact between the edges. Actually a slight gap is desirable. By slight I mean 1/16 inch at the most. Never force a gypsum wallboard into place. It will eventually buckle and warp if you do. Trim it to fit as closely as possible.

When you nail the wallboards to the ceiling, begin nailing from the center of the sheet and work out. This will prevent you from buckling the sheet as you fasten it.

Unless your wallboards extend from wall to wall without any butt joints, the butt joints should be staggered in the manner depicted in Fig. 4-20. There are two major advantages to staggering the butt joints. First, because the butt joints will occur on different joists, the chances of them cracking due to framing movements are slim. The other advantage is the ease of finishing several short butt joints as opposed to finishing one or two long ones. Butt joints are more difficult to finish than valley joints. Limiting the length of the butt joint makes it less difficult to finish. Of course if your wallboards do span from wall to wall, you certainly wouldn't want to create any butt joints.

The recommended nailing pattern for gypsum wallboard is illustrated in Fig. 4-21. The dimensions in the figure are maximum values and should not be exceeded. Note that Fig. 4-21 depicts double-nailing. The double-nail pattern is what should be used on all wallboards (both on walls and ceilings). Double-nailed wallboards are stronger and easier to finish. On a 4-×-8-foot sheet, like the

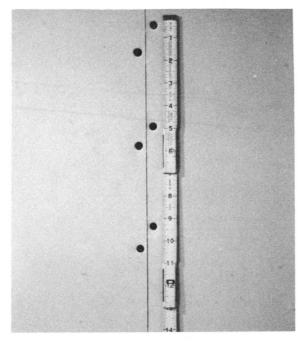

Fig. 4-22. Recommended nailing pattern for butt joints.

one shown in the Fig. 4-21, you drive three extra nails per sheet, yet you save 36 strokes of the joint knife during the joint finishing process when you fill in the nailhead dimples.

The nails on the butt joints should be offset by about 1 inch (as in Fig. 4-22). These nails must be dimpled carefully because they are so close to the edge of the wallboard. Offsetting the adjacent nails reduces the hazard of crushing the edge with the hammer. If the edge of the wallboard is damaged, the joint will be weak and difficult to finish.

When you are nailing the wallboards to the ceiling, don't stand directly under the nail you are driving and look up at it. Gypsum dust might fall in your eyes as the nail penetrates the core of the wallboard. The dust won't injure your eyes, but it will sure burn for a few minutes.

DRYWALLING THE WALLS

Once the ceiling is covered you can begin to drywall the walls. Doing the walls is similar in many re-

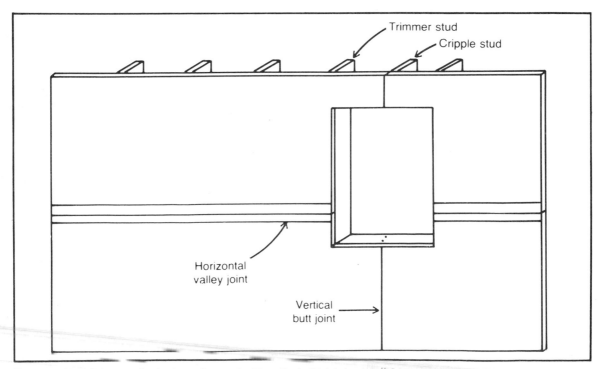

Fig. 4-23. Wall coverage using horizontal coursing. Since the butt joints land on the rough opening, butt joint staggering is not necessary.

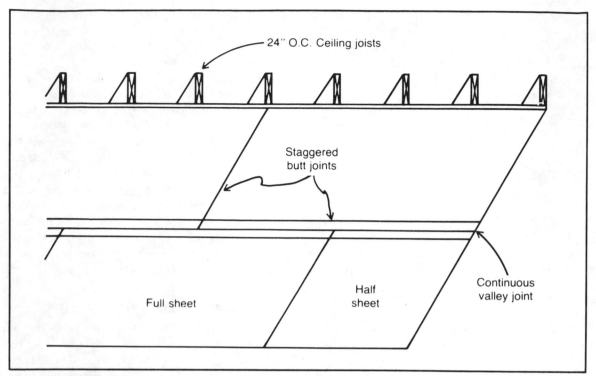

Fig. 4-20. Recommended method of ceiling coverage with butt joints staggered 4 feet apart.

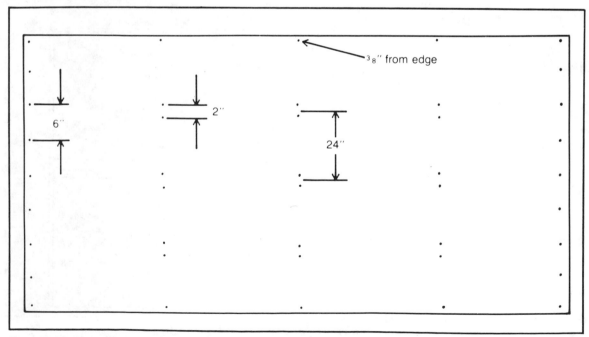

Fig. 4-21. Recommended nailing pattern for gypsum wallboard.

spects to doing the ceilings. The same nailing and gluing patterns are used on both walls and ceilings.

The wallboards on the walls can run either horizontally or vertically. By far the best method of covering the wall is to hang the sheets horizontally.

This is called *horizontal coursing*. See Fig. 4-23. As with ceilings, you should use the longest wallboards possible to reduce the number of butt joints.

There are distinct advantages to horizontal coursing on the walls. Note the horizontal valley

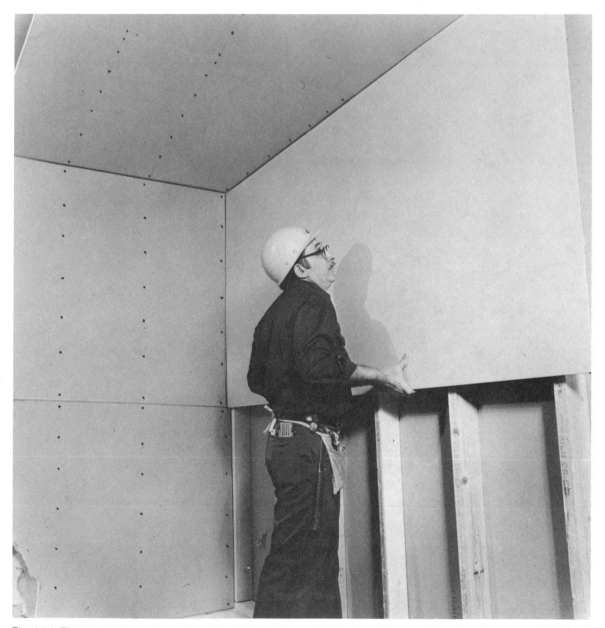

Fig. 4-24. The wallboards on the wall must be butted firmly under the edges of those on the ceiling (courtesy of the United States Gypsum Company).

joint in Fig. 4-23. It occurs 4 feet high and runs continuously around the perimeter of the wall. Such a joint is very easy to finish. It is at a convenient height and runs in a direction requiring no reaching at all. Also, experience has shown that the butt joints will most often occur at a rough opening, making them short and also very easy to finish. If the butt joints don't fall on rough openings, stagger them as you would for a ceiling. Here again, two short butt joints are easier to finish than one long one.

As you cover the walls, don't try to save a few dollars worth of wallboard by using scraps or remnants around rough openings. You will only make more work for yourself later on when you have to finish the extra joints you've created. The joints

around rough openings are also more apt to crack, especially if they join small pieces together. Use a full sheet, and cut the opening out of it, even if it means sacrificing half the sheet. In the long run it's really not a sacrifice; it's money well spent.

Always hang the top course first. Butt the edge of the wallboard firmly up under the edge of the ceiling sheet as is being done in Fig. 4-24. The corner formed at the wall and ceiling joint is the only place you should make firm contact between sheets.

Begin nailing the sheet from the top or close to it and work down. This way, if the wallboard is buckled from being pushed up, it will flatten out as you nail it down.

Once the top course is up, the bottom course can be hung. Always finish the top course before

Fig. 4-25. A curved light housing being drywalled with gypsum wallboard (courtesy of the United States Gypsum Company).

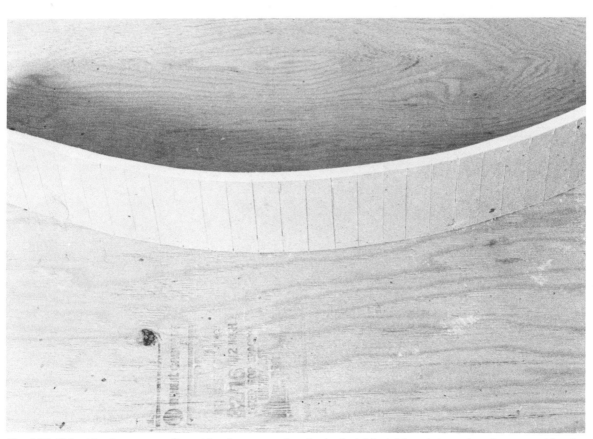

Fig. 4-26. This strip of gypsum wallboard has been scored on the back at 1-inch intervals to conform to a curved framing surface.

you start the bottom. If your wall is less than 8 feet tall (building codes allow 7-foot-6-inch minimum height) you will have to cut the bottom sheets. The edge you cut should be placed against the floor. If it's ragged or a bit short, it will be hidden behind the baseboard molding. When you position the wallboards in the bottom course, make light contact at the valley joint where the courses meet. Again, a slight gap is desirable. Nail the sheets in the bottom course from the top down, flattening them as you go.

DRYWALLING CURVED SURFACES

Almost any curved surface can be covered with gypsum wallboard. See Fig. 4-25. For mild curves, the wallboards can simply be pressed into place. Wetting gypsum wallboards thoroughly with a hose

and allowing them to soak for an hour will let you bend them to even tighter curves. Once the wallboard dries, it regains its original hardness but retains the curve. The wallboard is hung wet and allowed to dry in place; however, the wallboard must be hung very carefully to prevent damaging it.

For very tight curves, such as those in arched doorways, the method of drywall application is as follows. Score the back of the piece to be hung at 1-inch intervals like the strip shown in Fig. 4-26. Gently snap the cuts and bend the piece slightly as in Fig. 4-26.

Prior to nailing the piece in place, ensure that adequate nailing surfaces exist in the structure. Refer to Fig. 4-27 (the arched doorway). The ½-inch plywood on the two wall surfaces provides the nailing surface for the scored strip of wallboard.

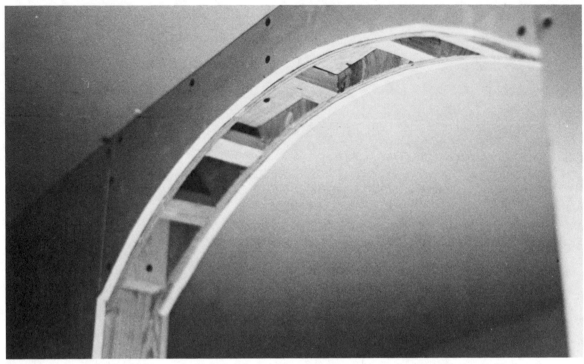

Fig. 4-27. A properly framed door arch. Note the plywood forms and the 2×1 spacing blocks between the forms.

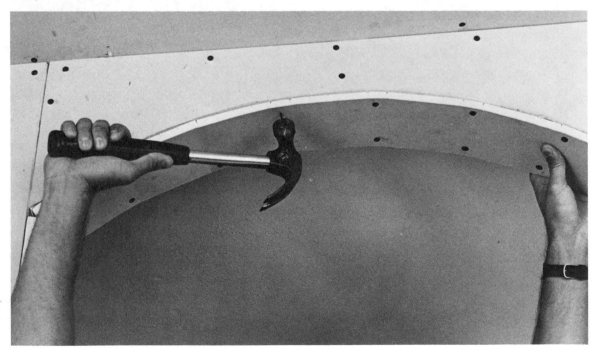

Fig. 4-28. Nailing a scored strip of gypsum wallboard to the forms of a curved door arch.

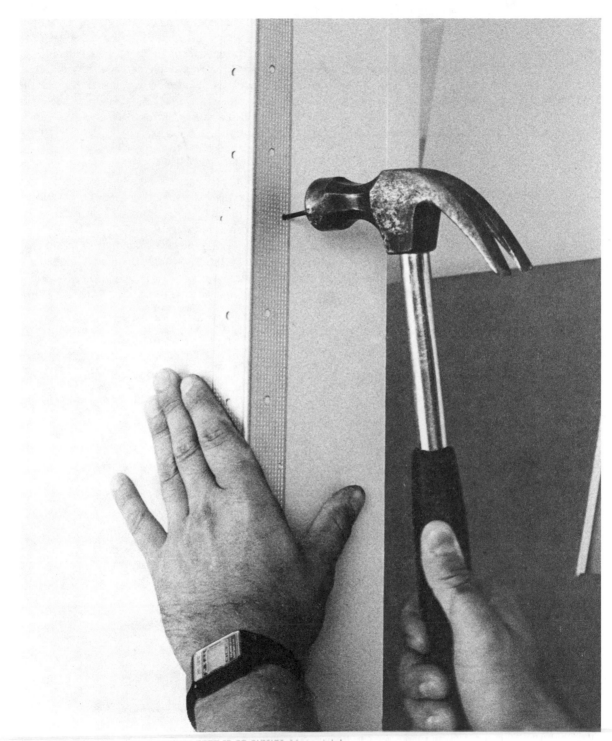

Fig. 4-13. Fastening a metal corner bead to an outside corner joint.

The blocks between the plywood provide structural support for the arch and will help prevent the doorway joints from cracking in the future.

To drywall the arch, press the scored panel into place and nail it on the edges at 4-inch intervals (Fig. 4-28). Drive the nails through solid portions of the curved wallboard (not through the cuts). Dimple the nailheads no more than is absolutely necessary. Take care not to smash the wallboard. It is a good idea to both glue and nail curved wallboard in place.

REINFORCING CORNERS

Metal corner beads must be placed over all outside corners before the outside corner joints can be properly finished. When installing corner beads, hold them firmly against the wallboards as shown in Fig. 4-29. Don't mash them down too flat though. The bead should stand out from the walls a bit so it

can be buried under joint compound. Place the nails close to the outside edge of the bead flanges. You can drive the nails through the prepunched holes or drive them directly through the flange as you see fit. Space the nails about 6 inches apart. Dimple the edge of the bead slightly as you drive the nails "home." Be careful not to nick the round corner of the bead with the hammer.

If you must butt the ends of two corner beads together, align them as carefully and accurately as you can. Place the factory-cut edges together. They will be straighter and smoother than you or I can cut them. If you must cut a corner bead, use either tin snips or aviation shears.

To bead a corner that is smaller or larger than 90 degrees at the angle, bend the flanges of the bead to fit the corner and nail it in place. All outside corners should be covered with a corner bead no

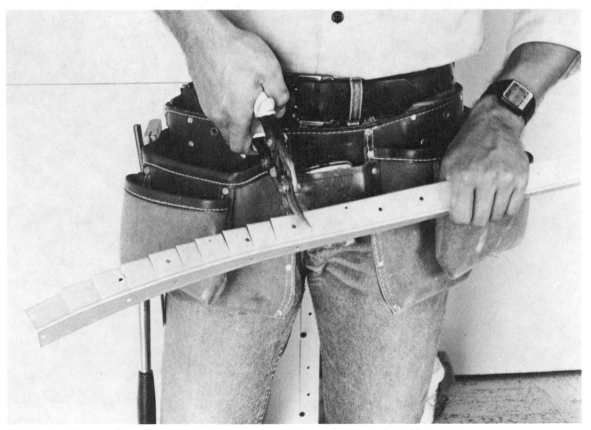

Fig. 4-30. Cutting one flange of a metal corner bead for application to a curved outside corner.

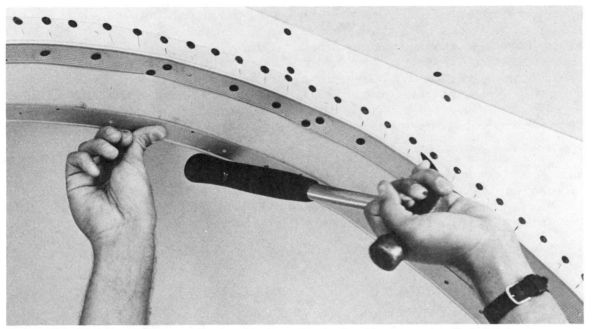

Fig. 4-31. Tapping a corner bead onto a curved outside corner. By using the rubber hammer handle, the bead can be properly seated without damaging it.

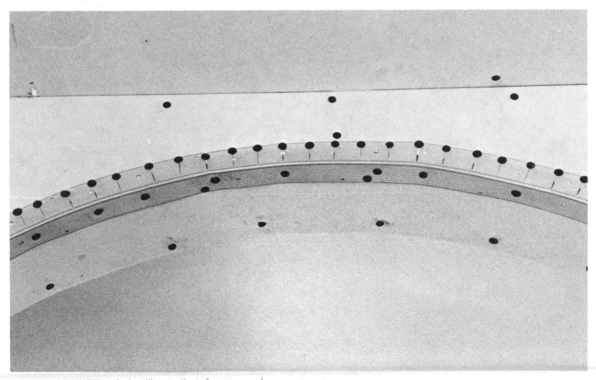

Fig. 4-32. Recommended nailing pattern for a curved corner bead.

63

matter how slight the angle.

Corner beads must also be applied to curved corners such as those occurring in doorway arches. To bead such a corner, snip the corner bead at 1-inch intervals on one flange (Fig. 4-30). As shown in Fig. 4-30, even as the bead is being snipped, it begins to curve. Next, press the corner bead over the corner joint. Striking the edge of the bead with a rubber mallet or hammer handle, as in Fig. 4-31, helps to seat the corner bead properly and form it into a smooth, consistent curve without damaging the bead.

Note the nailing pattern shown in Fig. 4-32. On the uncut flange of the bead, the nails are placed at 4- to 6-inch intervals. On the flange that was cut, the corners of the cuts are pinned down by the nailheads. This not only holds the bead in place, but also makes the joint easy to finish and helps prevent the corner joint from cracking in the future.

The corner bead on a curve can also be glued in place. Once all the nails are driven, wipe the bead clean of excess glue.

When drywalling, as with any other construction project, you should occasionally stop and admire your work. Not only will it give you confidence, but it will afford you the opportunity to find and correct any mistakes you made before they come back to haunt you later on.

Chapter 5

Joint Finishing

Once the joints of your drywall are ready for finishing, you face the most crucial task of all. No phase of drywall construction affects the appearance of the finished job more than joint finishing.

Taping and finishing the joints has traditionally been a very frustrating part of drywall construction, but it doesn't have to be. It can be very rewarding and even fun. Drywall joint finishing is basically a three-part process. You begin by applying a filler coat of joint compound to the nailheads and joints and then you reinforce them with paper joint tape. After the filler coat is dry it is sanded down. Next, the joints are coated and sanded again. Finally, a watered down, or "tempered" finish coat of joint compound is applied. A good finish coat requires no sanding. That's all there is to it.

The best order to follow in joint finishing is: nailheads, valley joints, inside corners, corner beads, and butt joints. This way you start with the easiest and end with the hardest. By the time you get to the butt joints, you will have developed some finesse with the joint knives and won't find them too difficult to finish. You should give the

joints and nailheads a filler coat all at once. After 24 hours, give them all a second coat. The finish coat can be applied 24 hours after the second coat has been applied.

BEFORE YOU START

As with wallboard hanging, there are some things you must check prior to finishing your joints. The first thing to check for is excessive space between wallboards. A slight gap between wallboards is desirable, but there is a limit. Gaps between wallboards that approach ¼ inch should be filled with joint compound and allowed to dry for 24 hours before the filler coat is applied. Gaps of ½ inch or more should be filled with a strip of wallboard glued in place. It is a good idea to let the glue dry overnight before applying the filler coat to the joint.

Next, make sure there are no loose wallboards. Some of your nails might have loosened from hammering, and especially if the wallboard was nailed to furring strips. Check the centers and especially the edges of the wallboards by pushing on them. Watch for movement around the fasteners.

Check the ceilings very closely. If the wallboards show any signs of looseness, double up on the nails. Of course if you also glued the sheets up, this won't be a problem. The glue will hold them fast.

In Chapter 6 there is an excellent drywall problem diagnosis and repair guide that also outlines preventive measures. Look through the guide and try to identify any potential problem areas in the drywall system before you begin to finish the joints.

HANDLING JOINT KNIVES AND JOINT COMPOUND

Finishing your joints will be much easier if you follow the tips I give you here. The first thing you should do when you open a bucket of joint compound or "mud" is scrape the inside of the lid and wash it clean of mud. If you don't do this, the mud that's left on the lid will dry and crumble. The particles will fall into the fresh mud and get caught on the end of your joint knife, leaving gouges in your joints as you try to skim them smooth. Always keep the bucket closed tightly when you are not actually filling your mud pan.

Be very careful how you handle your joint knives. Don't allow the edges of the blades to become nicked or bent. Once this happens, the tool is useless and will never properly finish a joint again. Always wash your joint knives thoroughly after use. Don't allow dried joint compound to remain on them. Dry them completely. Don't put them away wet. Never soak them in water for long periods of time. The blades will rust, the rivets will pop, and the wooden handles will crack. A good set of joint knives will last a lifetime if properly cared for.

Keep some water handy when you finish the

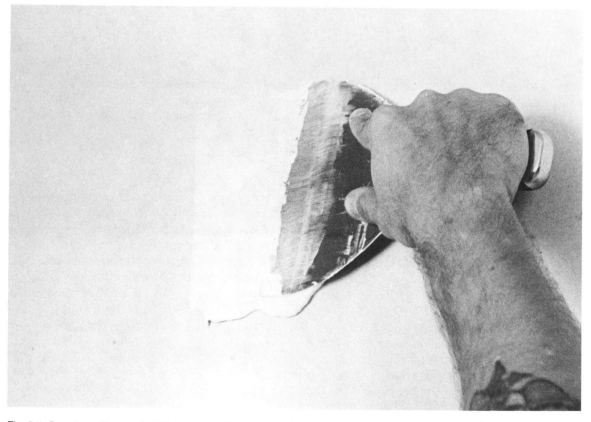

Fig. 5-1. Pressing a filler coat of joint compound into a pair of nailheads. Note the low angle at which the blade is held to the wallboard.

Fig. 5-2. Scraping the excess joint compound away from the nailheads that were filled in Fig. 5-1. No excess joint compound is left on the face of the wallboard. Note that the blade is held at a steep angle to the wallboard.

joints. If you get a lot of dry mud built up on your joint knives, wash them off. The dried mud will crumble off into your mud pan and complicate things as you try to skim the joints smooth. Frequently scraping the knife blade clean on the edge of the mud pan can prevent this for the most part.

If you spill some mud on the floor as you are applying it to the joints, wipe it up as soon as possible. Even if it dries on the floor, it can still be cleaned off easily. If you step in it while it is wet, you might slip and injure yourself in a fall.

APPLYING THE FILLER COAT

Begin the joint finishing process by filling in the nailheads on the walls. Starting there will give you a chance to become familiar with the joint knife and the mud in a place where you can't mess up the job too much.

Using a 6-inch joint knife, fill your mud pan about half full. Scoop out about an inch of mud; that's about enough to fill a pair of nailheads without falling off the blade. Press the mud into the nailheads as shown in Fig. 5-1. Notice that the blade of the knife is held at a low angle to the wallboard surface. This is done so that the mud is compressed into the nailhead dimple as much as possible. Next, scrape the excess mud from the wallboard surface. Do this in a direction 90 degrees from that in which you applied it, as in Fig. 5-2. Hold the blade at a 45-degree angle to the wallboard surface so that all the mud except that left in the dimple is scraped away. Do not leave a buildup of mud on the wallboard surface. A properly filled nailhead is filled flush with the wallboard surface and requires no sanding. If you find any nailheads too close to the surface of the wallboard, drive them deep enough to be covered completely with mud. Once you have filled the nailheads on the walls, do the ones on the ceiling. You will have to hold the mud pan under your joint knife until you get the knack of smearing it onto the ceiling.

As you are finishing the nailheads, look for dents and scrapes in the wallboard surfaces. Fill them and scrape them flush just as you would a nailhead. Also fill in any gaps around electrical boxes (Fig. 5-3). Fill in such gaps completely and scrape them flush with the wallboard surface. It is important that you completely seal the box into the hole. This will prevent any sparks from entering the wall cavity and causing a fire.

After the nailheads and electrical boxes get their first coat, start finishing the valley joints on the walls. Begin by generously filling the valley with mud. Use a 6-inch joint knife as shown in Fig.

5-4. Press the mud into the joint so it is forced into the gap between the sheets. If you coursed the wallboards vertically, fill them from the top and bottom toward the center so you don't spill mud all over the floor. Note in Fig. 5-4 that the blade is held at a low angle to the wallboard surface. This is done so that the mud is pressed firmly into the joint. Fill the entire length of the valley.

Next, cut a piece of joint tape the length of the joint. Starting at one end of the joint, press the tape into the mud with your fingers. Then, using a 6-inch joint knife, press the tape into the bottom of the valley and flatten it out as in Fig. 5-5. Hold the tape on the end so it doesn't move. Hold the blade at a very low angle to the wallboard so it conforms to the curve of the valley and presses the tape in deeply enough to be buried in mud under the wallboard surface. Press the tape down firmly until it adheres

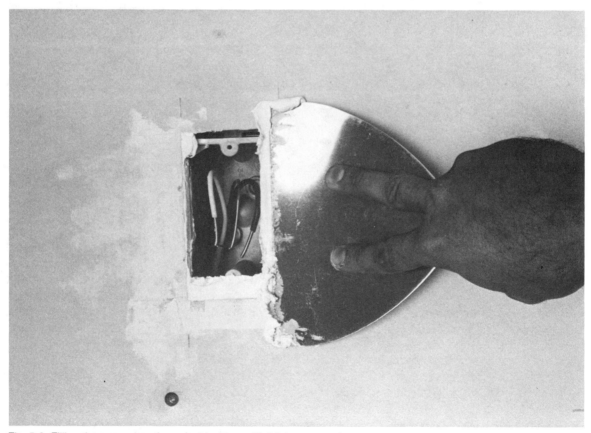

Fig. 5-3. Filling the gaps around an electrical box with joint compound.

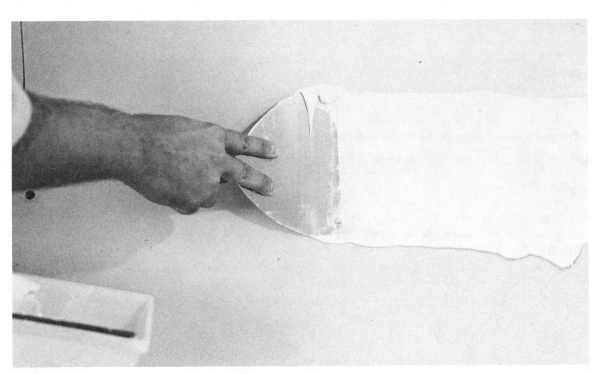

Fig. 5-4. Applying the filler coat of joint compound to a valley joint.

Fig. 5-5. Pressing the joint tape into the filler coat of a valley joint. Note the finger placed in the center of the blade which forces the blade to conform to the curve of the valley.

69

to the wallboard, but not so firmly that you squeeze all the joint compound out from under the joint tape.

Once the tape is in place, apply another coat of joint compound over the joint. Cover the tape completely, as in Fig. 5-6, but don't fill the valley completely. If you fill the valley completely, it would require more than 24 hours to dry. Worse yet, it might crack open during drying. In the event it does crack, all is not lost. You can simply ignore it and fill it in again, but the chances of it cracking after it is finished will be greater.

After the tape is covered, scrape the excess mud from the wallboard surface. You can use either a 6-inch or 12-inch joint knife to do this, but the 12-inch knife is best.

If the joint tape doesn't adhere well to the wallboard, fix it while the joint compound is still workable. Don't leave any bubbles or blisters under

the tape. After you fill in the valleys on the walls, do the ones on the ceiling. Should you have any extremely long joints to finish, you can do them in 8-foot lengths. If you do, make sure you overlap the ends of the joint tape at least 3 inches on the ends and adhere them together with plenty of mud.

The inside corners on the walls are a good place to go to next. You won't need the 6-inch joint knife or the mud pan to do the inside corner joints. Take the mud right out of the bucket with a corner trowel. Coat the joint generously with mud. Press the mud firmly into the joint as shown in Fig. 5-7. Fill the joint from both ends toward the center so you don't end up with a pile of mud on the floor at the bottom of the joint. Next, cut a piece of tape long enough to cover the joint. Carefully fold the joint tape along the center crease as in Fig. 5-8. Take care to fold the tape evenly. Press the tape into the

Fig. 5-6. Covering the joint tape in a valley joint with joint compound. Note that the finger is not used to curve the blade this time.

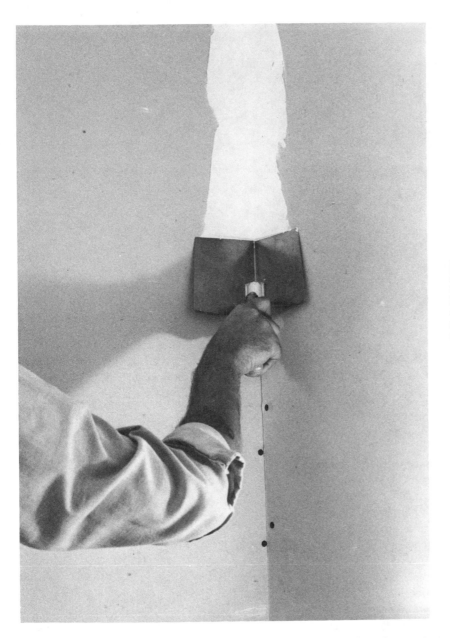

Fig. 5-7. Filling in inside corner joint with joint compound using a corner trowel. The blade is held at a low angle so the joint compound is pressed into the nailheads and the gap between the wallboards.

joint while carefully aligning the fold with the joint, then flatten it into the joint with the corner trowel. Press the tape firmly into the joint, but don't squeeze out all the joint compound from under it. Make sure the tape thoroughly adheres to the wallboard. This is especially important at the edges. If it doesn't adhere, lift it up and smear some more joint compound under it.

After the tape is satisfactorily embedded in the joint, cover it completely with more mud and skim it smooth as shown in Fig. 5-9. The tape shouldn't show through at all. Here again don't leave so much mud on the joint that it invites cracking or excessive drying time. Use a 6-inch joint knife to remove any excess mud at the edges of the joint. After the inside corners on the walls are done, fill the ones on the

Fig. 5-8. Carefully folding a piece of paper joint tape along the center crease for application to an inside corner joint.

ceiling. Long corner joints can also be done in 8-foot steps, providing the ends of the tape are overlapped and adhered well with joint compound.

Move on to the corner beads once you finish filling and taping the inside corners. As usual, start with those on the walls first. Corner beads are very easy to finish. Using the 6-inch joint knife, generously fill the bead flanges one at a time with mud. Use the rounded nose of the bead as a guide for the knife blade as shown in Fig. 5-10. Hold the knife at a low angle to the wallboard so that the mud is pressed firmly into the bead flange, the prepunched holes, and the edges of the flange. As shown in Fig. 5-10, note how the joint knife is held. The index finger is far back from the edge of the blade. The blade curves very little, allowing a thick enough coat of mud to remain on the bead flange.

Once the bead is full, scrape away the excess mud. You can use a 6-inch or 12-inch joint knife. If you use a 12-inch knife, as shown in Fig. 5-11, the result will be a well-feathered joint after only the first coat. Skim the joint smooth from the top and

Fig. 5-9. Burying the joint tape in an inside corner joint.

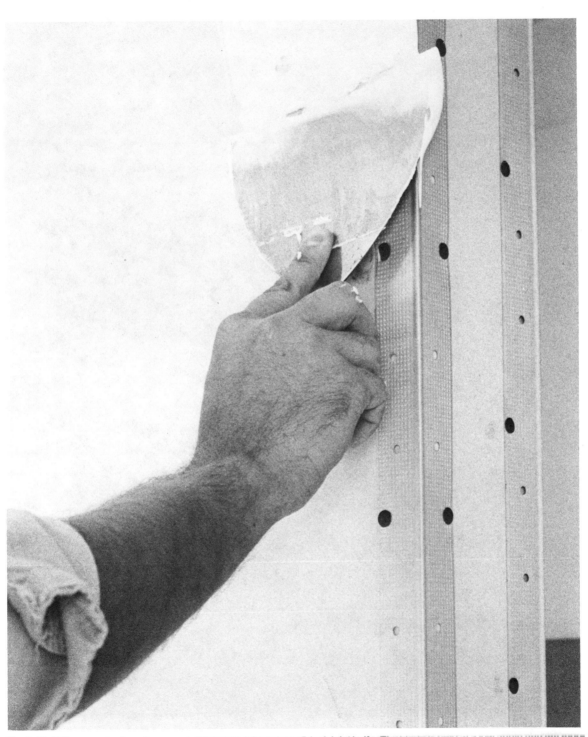

Fig. 5-10. Filling a corner bead on an outside corner joint using a 6-inch joint knife. The blade is held at a low angle and the bead edge is used as a form for the blade to ensure proper filling.

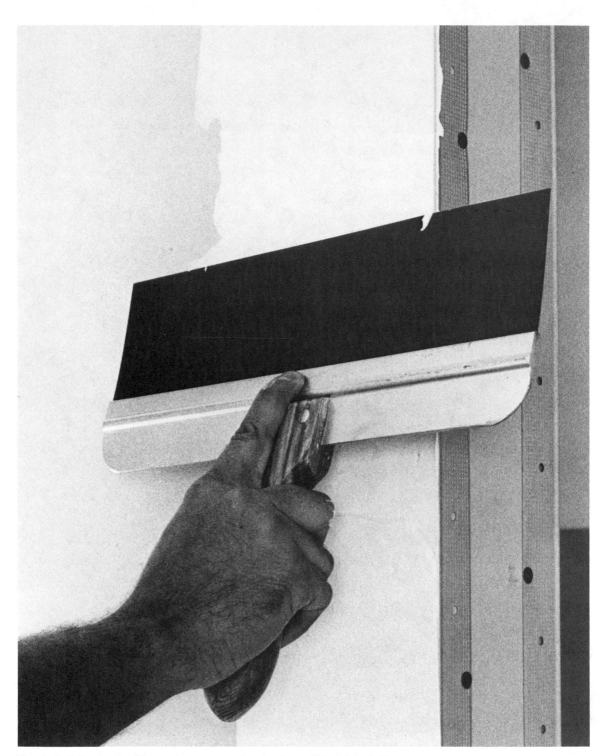

Fig. 5-11. Skimming the filler coat on a corner bead using a 12-inch joint knife.

bottom toward the center to keep the mud off the floor.

Fill and smooth the corner bead one flange at a time. Don't worry about removing the excess mud from the bead edge. It will sand off easily enough after it dries. You will only risk nicking the blade of your joint knife if you try to scrape the bead clean with it. A properly filled corner bead is shown in Fig. 5-12.

At this point, the only joints left to fill are the butt joints. If the wallboard was properly hung, the butt joints should only be 4 feet wide. Once again start on the walls. Generously coat the butt joint with mud. Smear on a good, thick coat (as in Fig. 5-13) with a 6-inch joint knife. Next, cut a piece of

Fig. 5-13. Applying a heavy filler coat to a butt joint using a 6-inch joint knife. The blade is held at a low angle but not too much pressure is applied.

joint tape long enough to cover the joint. Press the tape into the mud with your fingers. Once it is in place, flatten it into the joint with the 6-inch joint knife. There should be enough mud on the joint so that as you flatten the tape it is almost covered over and doesn't show through. See Fig. 5-14.

Cover the tape on the butt joint with another thick layer of mud. Now skim it smooth with a curved joint trowel. Hold the blade of the trowel at a very low angle to the wallboard and, with moderate pressure, draw it down the joint as in Fig. 5-15. The curvature of the trowel will produce a crown in the joint that will hide the tape and feather the edges quite nicely. The edges don't have to be too smooth on the first coat. The most important thing is to hide

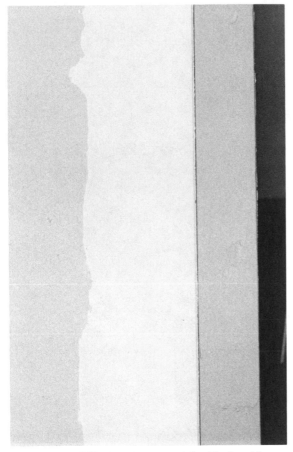

Fig. 5-12. A well-filled outside corner joint. The bead flanges are completely hidden under the joint compound, but the nose remains exposed.

takes 24 hours for most drying types of joint compounds.

The best way to sand the joints is with a pole sander. Use #100-grit sandpaper. Anything more coarse will roughen the facing paper of the wallboard and cause problems during painting. Always wear a dust mask and block off any cold-air return vents in the area in which you are sanding. You don't want the dust circulating into the rest of your house through the heating or cooling system.

You shouldn't have to sand the nailheads if you filled them in properly. Just the same, look for any with too much mud on them and sand them off flush with the wallboard surface.

You can begin sanding anywhere you choose. I usually start with the valley and butt joints on the

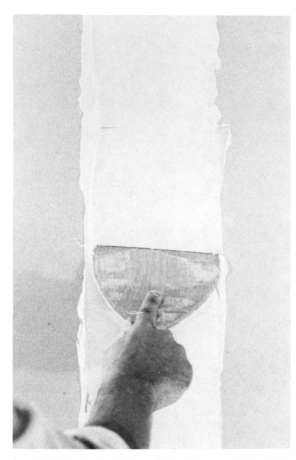

Fig. 5-14. Burying the joint tape in the filler coat of a butt joint. Note that the tape doesn't show through.

the tape completely under the mud.

If you don't have a curved joint trowel, you can still finish the butt joints using a 12-inch joint knife. After burying the tape with mud, skim the joint smooth with the 12-inch knife. Then feather each edge separately also using the 12-incher. Be sure the tape remains well hidden under the mud.

APPLYING THE SECOND COAT

Applying the second coat of mud to the joints will be much easier than the first. You won't have to do any taping and you won't use nearly as much mud. But before you can apply the second coat, you must sand the filler coat. The filler coat will be ready for sanding once it is completely dry. That usually

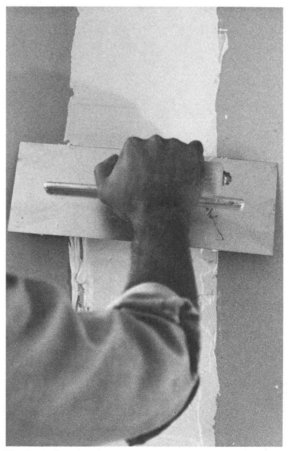

Fig. 5-15. Creating the proper crown on a butt joint filler coat with a curved drywall trowel.

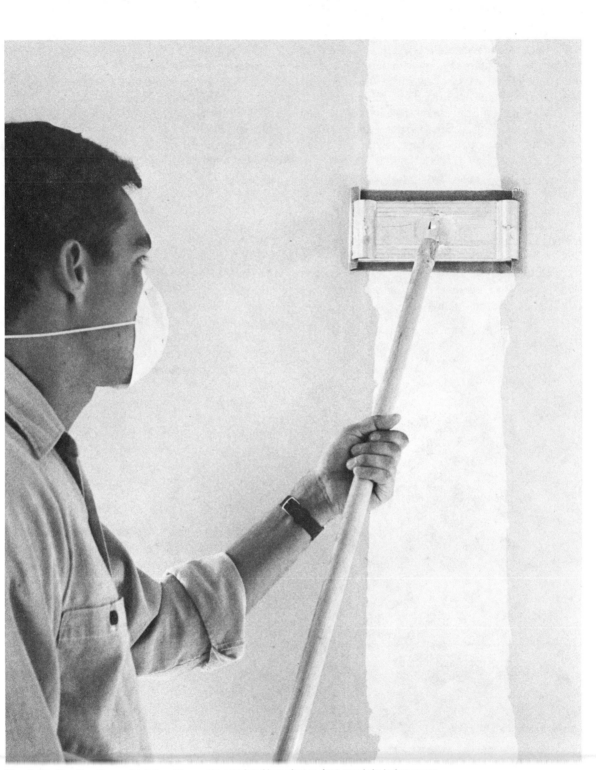

Fig. 5-16. Sanding the wall joints with a pole sander. Note that a dust mask is being worn.

walls because they are the easiest to sand. Hold the pole sander and start sanding with light pressure as shown in Fig. 5-16. Stroke the sander along the length of the joint, but float the sanding head from edge to edge. Concentrate on the edges of the joint more than the center. Spot sand any lumps or depressions in the joint. The edges are the crucial part of the joint. Try to feather them as smoothly as possible. The best way to check the edges of the joint is by running your hand across the joint as in Fig. 5-17. Move your fingertips across the joint. You should feel no ridge or change of surface where the edge of the joints meets the wallboard. If you do, the joint needs more sanding or filling with joint compound. Sand the edges of the joints as smooth as you can without sanding down to the joint tape. Check the edges frequently as you sand the joints.

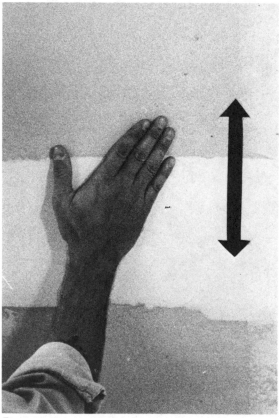

Fig. 5-17. Checking the smoothness of the feathered edge of a wall joint. By moving your hand in the direction of the arrow, you can feel how smoothly the joint blends into the wallboard.

Corner beads are also sanded with the pole sander. Use the bead edge as a guide for the sanding head (Fig. 5-18). You can apply a bit more pressure to the sanding head on the corner beads, but don't sand too deeply. Concentrate on feathering out the edges of the joint. Check the bead with your hand frequently during sanding. Sand the excess mud from the rounded bead nose with a handheld piece of sandpaper.

For sanding inside corners, an angle sander is very handy. An angle sander is being used to sand the inside corner. See Fig. 5-19. When sanding an inside corner, don't apply too much pressure to the sanding head. Let the sandpaper do the work. It is very easy to oversand an inside corner joint before you realize you've done it. The planes of the angle sander are spring loaded. By applying light pressure, most of the sanding will occur at the edges where it is most needed. If you don't have an angle sanding head, you can still sand the inside corners with a flat sanding head by sanding one side of the joint at a time.

After you finish sanding down the wall joints, sand the ones on the ceiling. Once you are finished sanding, completely dust off all the joints, wall, and ceiling surfaces. A broom works well for this. After you have dusted everything off, you can apply the second coat of mud to the joints.

APPLYING THE SECOND COAT

Apply the second coat of mud in the same order as the first; nailheads, valley joints, inside corners, corner beads, and butt joints. You won't have to coat the gaps around the electrical boxes again as long as they were completely filled in the first time.

The second coat is applied primarily for cosmetic purposes. Almost all of the structural bonding is provided by the filler coat. Try to apply the second coat as smoothly as you can, but if it doesn't come out too smooth don't be discouraged. You will have to sand it down anyway before applying the finish coat.

Fill the nailheads with mud again in exactly the same manners as you did for the filler coat. Remember to scrape them off flush at the surface. Do not leave a buildup of mud around the dimple.

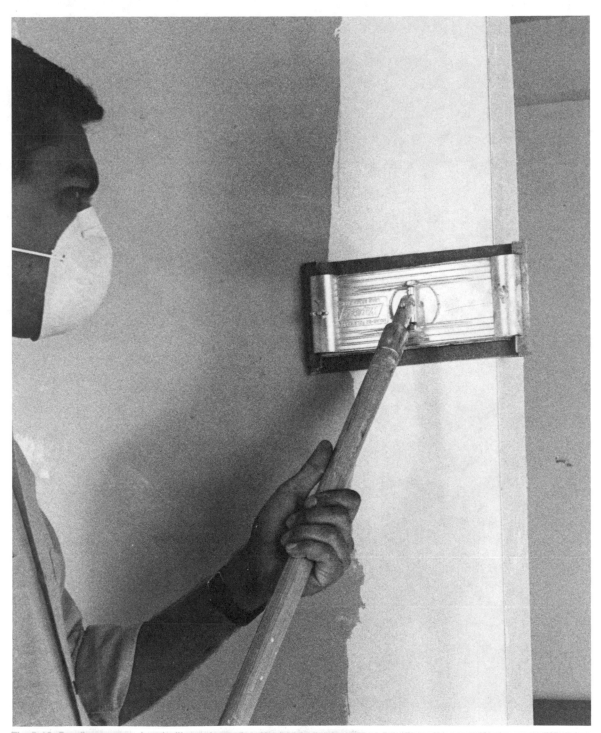

Fig. 5-10. Sanding a corner bead with a pole sander. The bead edge is used as a guide for the sanding pan so the joint is not oversanded.

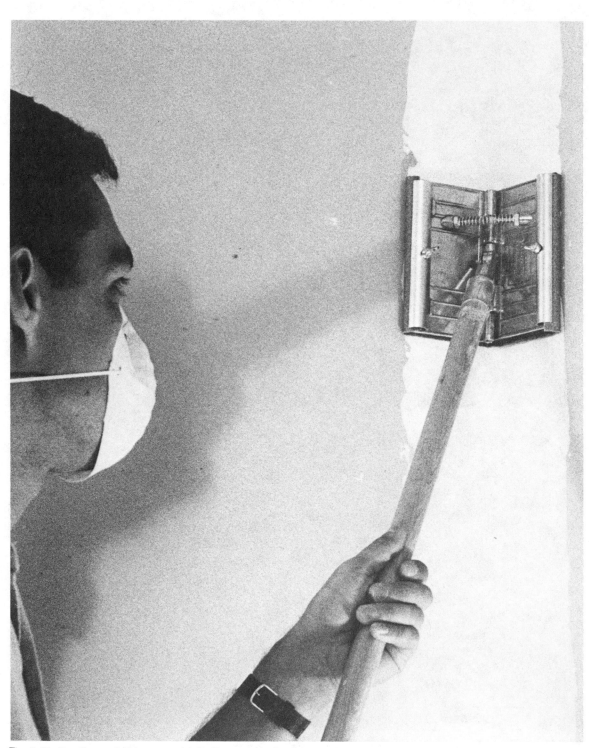

Fig. 5-19. Sanding an inside corner joint with an angle sander.

Next move on to the valley joints. Using a 6-inch joint knife, apply a coat of mud over the valley. Skim the joint smooth using a 12-inch joint knife as in Fig. 5-20. Hold the knife at about a 30-degree angle as you draw it along the joint, preventing the blade from curving into the valley too much. As shown in Fig. 5-20, the second coat is feathered a bit wider than the filler coat even though it was applied with a 6-inch knife. The 12-inch knife spreads it wider and effectively gauges the coat thickness as you draw it along the joint. You can also use a curved-joint trowel to finish valley joints, but a 12-inch flat joint knife produces a much better valley joint.

You might experience some cratering in the mud when applying the second coat, but that's acceptable. Don't waste a lot of time trying to fill the craters in while you are applying the second coat. It is much easier to let them dry and fill them in with the finish coat.

Next do the inside corner joints. Using the corner trowel, fill the inside corner joint with a coat of mud. Clean off the trowel and use it to skim the coat smooth. Beads of mud left at the edges of the joint can be craped away with a 6-inch joint knife, but take care not to disturb the feathered edge of the joint while you are doing it.

After coating the inside corners, do the corner beads on the outside corner joints. The second coat

is applied to the corner beads exactly the same way as the filler coat. Apply the mud with a 6-inch joint knife and skim it smooth with a 12-incher. It's not a good idea to use a curved joint trowel on corner beads. It doesn't finish them flat enough.

Now apply the second coat of mud to the butt joints. Apply a thick coat of mud to the joint with a 12-inch joint knife. Then use a curved joint trowel to skim the joint smooth as shown in Fig. 5-21. If the edges of the joint don't feather out properly, coat the joint with more mud and skim it off again. Note in the figure how much wider the second coat is than the filler coat. Use the 6-inch joint knife to scrape away the beads of mud left at the edges of the joint without disturbing the feathered edges.

APPLYING THE FINISH COAT

The finish coat is the last coat of mud applied to the joints before the wallboard is painted. You have no doubt guessed that you must sand the second coat before you can apply the finish coat. Sand the joints down again just as you did before. If your second coat came out fairly smooth, not much sanding will be required. Again, concentrate on feathering out the edges of the joints during sanding. After you sand them all down, be sure to remove all of the dust before applying the finish coat.

The finish coat should be applied with mud that is watered down some. The added water will improve the smoothness of the finish coat and reduce the tendency of the mud to crater during application. In fact, a properly applied finish coat requires no sanding at all after it dries.

To water down or "temper" the joint compound for the finish coat, add small amounts of water to the mud after it is in the mud pan. Don't water down the mud in the bucket. Mix it up well but not so well that it foams up. Don't work a lot of air bubbles into it. Air bubbles cause cratering. Don't add too much water. If the mud won't stay on the knife, it is too thin. Add some fresh mud to it to thicken it up.

Apply the finish coat using the same techniques you used to apply the second coat. Check your work carefully to make sure you have filled in all craters and feathered all joint edges. The

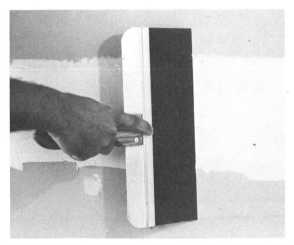

Fig. 5-20. Skimming the second coat on a valley joint smooth with a 12-inch joint knife.

Fig. 5-21. Skimming the second coat smooth on a butt joint with a curved joint trowel. Note how much wider the second coat is than the first.

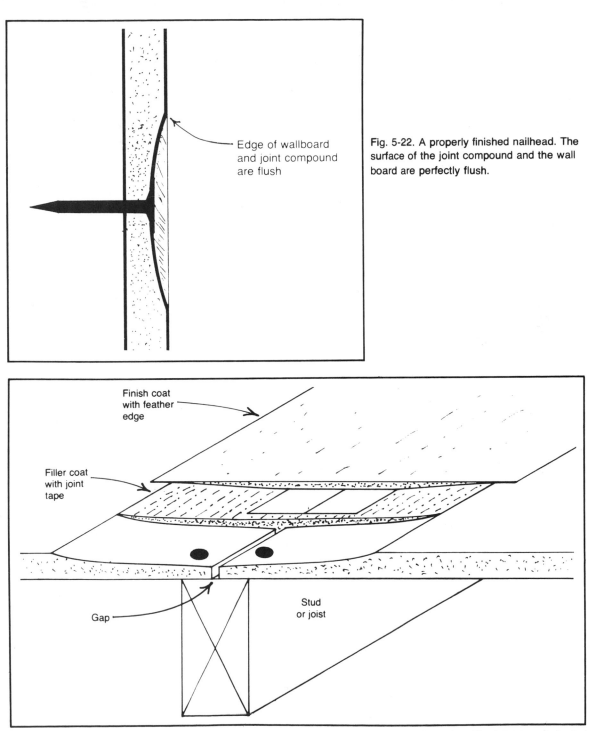

Fig. 5-22. A properly finished nailhead. The surface of the joint compound and the wall board are perfectly flush.

Edge of wallboard and joint compound are flush

Finish coat with feather edge

Filler coat with joint tape

Gap

Stud or joist

Fig. 5-23. A properly finished valley joint. The finish coat is feathered out to a very thin edge. The joint tape is buried well below the wallboard surface and the joint is finished flat with only a slight crown.

finish coat is thin and should dry rapidly under most conditions.

The purpose of the finish coat is purely cosmetic. If you spot imperfection in it, allow it to dry, and then either apply another tempered finish coat over it or touch it up in selected spots that need attention. If your finish coat requires sanding, use a fine grade of sandpaper (around #180 grit or finer). The tiny sanding lines won't show through the paint.

It is crucial that all joint edges be feathered as smoothly as possible. This is especially important on ceilings. When the joints show through a finished and painted drywall system, it is most often because the joint edges weren't feathered smoothly enough. Imperfections on ceilings show up more easily because of the way light strikes the joints. Figures 5-22 through 5-26 show the details of properly finished drywall joints and nailheads.

If you spot problems in your joints after you have painted your walls and ceilings, you can apply additional coats of mud right over the paint as long

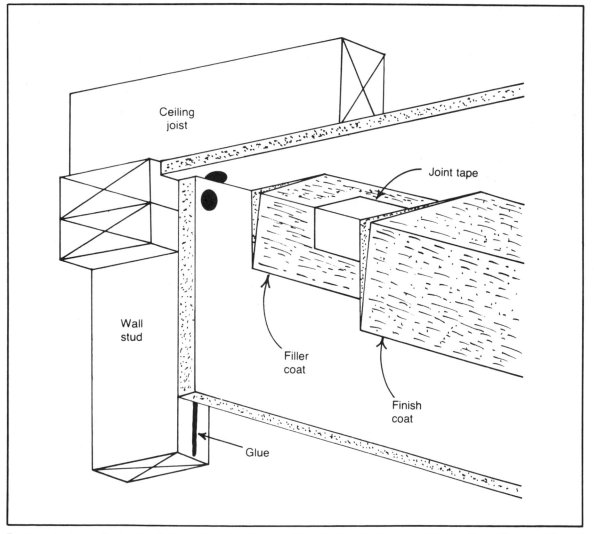

Fig. 5-24. A properly finished inside corner joint. The finish coat is wider than the filler coat. Note how the wallboard on the wall supports the edge of the one on the ceiling, also creating a very straight corner joint.

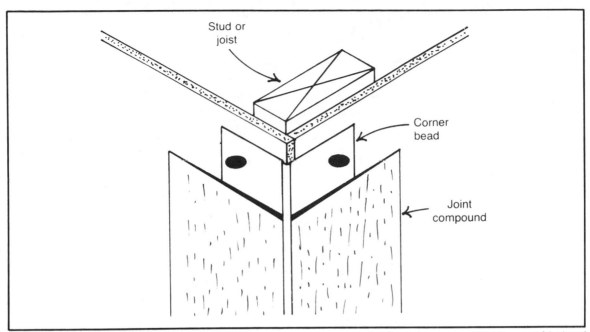

Fig. 5-25. A properly finished outside corner joint. The round nose of the corner bead remains exposed. The flanges of the bead are completely covered with joint compound that is feathered out to a very thin edge.

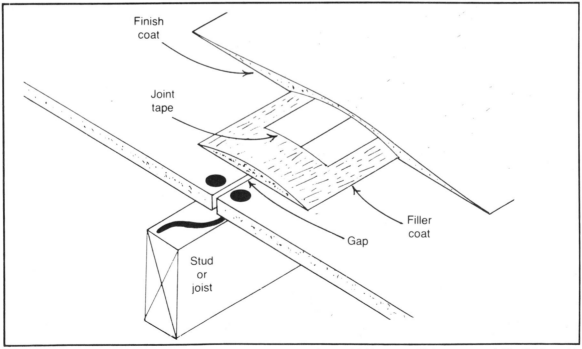

Fig. 5-26. A properly finished butt joint. The joint tape is well covered by the highly crowned joint compound. The finish coat is much wider than the filler coat and the edges are well-feathered to hide the joint on the wallboard surface.

as it is dry. Apply the mud and sand the joint just as if you were doing it over bare wallboard; then paint over it again.

Be sure you leave absolutely no sanding dust on the wallboard before you paint it. The first coat of paint might seem to go on all right, but the second coat of paint will peel the first coat right off the wall and onto your roller.

Bare gypsum wallboard normally requires no priming so long as a good-quality alkyd or latex paint is used. The dried joint compound will have the same absorption characteristics as the paper on the wallboard (especially if both were made by the same manufacturer).

Chapter 6
Drywall Repairs

Holes, dents, cracks, and joints that show through the paint detract from the appearance of any home. There is no reason to live with these nuisances. They can be repaired easily and inexpensively using joint compound and joint tape. Joint compound can be applied right over painted surfaces with little or no surface preparation. Joint compound can be purchased in a variety of containers ideally suited for small jobs such as repairs.

DAMAGED WALLBOARD

Small holes such as nail holes or holes left after wall anchors have been removed can be filled with a small tube of joint compound like that shown in Fig. 6-1. Simply squeeze some joint compound into the hole until it is filled. After the compound dries, sand it flush with the wallboard surface. Feel it with your fingertips to ensure that it is flush on the surface. Remember, joint compounds shrink as they dry. Refill and sand the hole until it is flush. Clean off the sanding dust and paint the spot you patched.

Very small holes and hairline cracks can be

filled in with a drywall and plaster-repair stick like the one shown in Fig. 6-2. Rub the stick across the hole or crack until it is completely filled in. After sanding the excess patching compound off the wallboard surface and brushing away the dust, the repaired area can be painted.

Dents and scratches in gypsum wallboard should be repaired with joint compound and a 6-inch joint knife. Use the joint knife to press the joint compound into the depression. Once it is filled, scrape it flush on the surface. This procedure is identical to the method of filling in nailhead dimples (described in Chapter 5). Sand and finish dents at least twice before painting them.

Areas where the wallboard has been punctured clear through must be taped. The hole shown in Fig. 6-3 was made with a hammer. The first step in repairing this hole is to remove all loose paper and gypsum particles from the hole. Trim the edges of the hole with a utility knife as shown in Fig. 6-5. Next, press plenty of joint compound into the hole with a 6-inch joint knife. Drag the blade of the knife

Fig. 6-1. Patching a small hole in gypsum wallboard with a tube of joint compound.

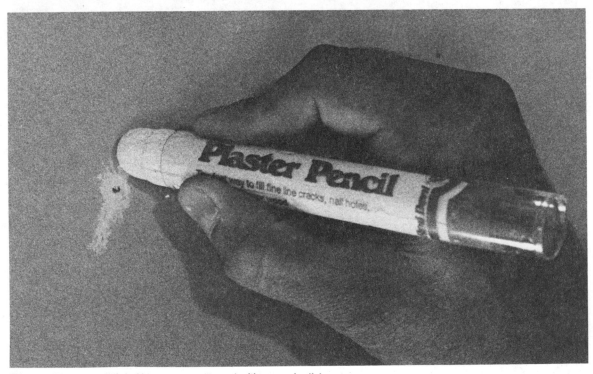

Fig. 6-2. Filling a nail hole in gypsum wallboard with a repair stick.

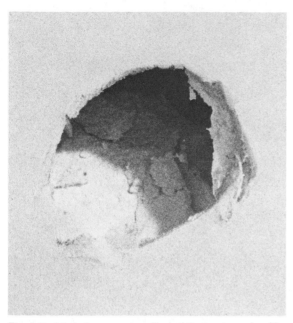

Fig. 6-3. A hole in gypsum wallboard that was made with a hammer.

in all four directions so that the mud sticks to the sides of the hole (as in Fig. 6-5).

Leave a fairly heavy coat of joint compound on the wallboard surface; don't scrape it off flush. Press a short piece of joint tape into the joint compound over the hole. Use the 6-inch joint knife to press it down smooth as shown in Fig. 6-6. Spread another coat of joint compound over the tape and press in a second piece of joint tape over the first. The second piece of tape should be placed perpendicularly to the first. Cover the entire area around the patch with more joint compound, feathering it out at the edges until it looks like the one shown in Fig. 6-7. Allow the joint compound to dry overnight. Once it's dry, sand it by hand with 100-grit sandpaper. Take care not to sand through to the joint tape or press too hard on the hole. Finish and sand the patch as many times as required to make it smooth. Once you are satisfied with it, paint it. If it shows through the paint, apply more mud to it and

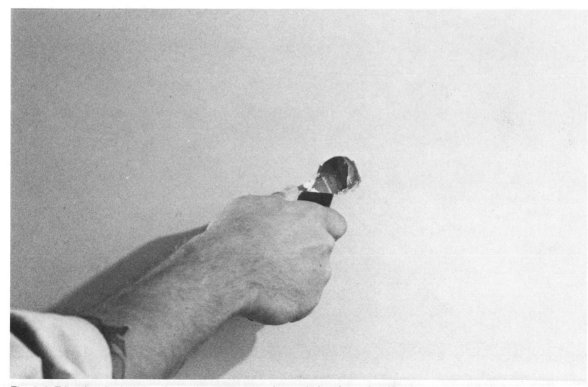

Fig. 6-4. Trimming the loose paper and gypsum away from a hole prior to repairing it.

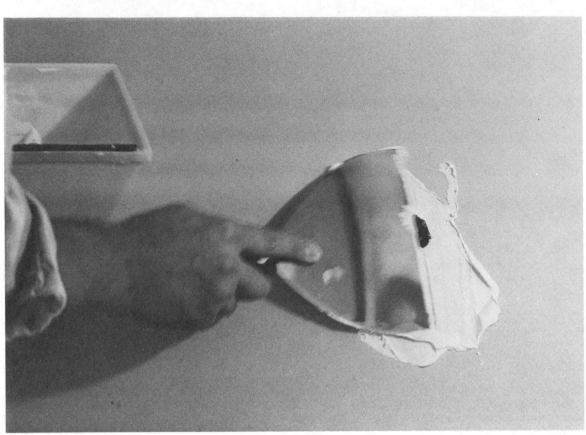

Fig. 6-5. Pressing joint compound into the hole. Note the coat of joint compound left on the wallboard surface around the hole.

sand it down again. You do not need to remove the paint first.

DEFECTIVE DRYWALL SYSTEMS

There are many reasons why problems develop in finished drywall systems. The remainder of this chapter is a diagnosis and repair guide. It was written by and provided here as a courtesy of the United States Gypsum Company.

Almost invariably, unsatisfactory results show up first in the areas over joints or fastener heads. Improper application of either the board or joint treatment *may* be at fault, but other conditions existing on the job can be equally responsible for reducing the quality of the finished gypsum board surface.

To help determine the exact problem cause, the physical appearance of each defect is described here along with a discussion of the factors causing unsatisfactory results. The checklist following contains possible causes for the irregularity and serves as an index to the numerically listed problems, causes, remedies, and preventions. By checking each numerical item listed for the defect, the exact problem cause can be determined and appropriate corrective action taken.

Description of Defect

Fastener Imperfections. A common defect which takes on many forms. May appear as darkening, localized cracking or a depression over fastener heads, pop or protrusion of the fastener or the surface area immediately surrounding the fastener. Usually caused by improper framing or application of fasteners.

Joint Defects. Generally occur in a straight-line pattern and appear as ridges, depressions, or blisters at the joints, or darkening over the joints or in adjacent panel areas. Imperfections may be result of incorrect framing or joint treatment, or climatic conditions if remedial action has not been taken.

Loose Panels. Board does not have tight contact with framing, rattles when impacted or moves when pressure is applied to the surface. Caused by improper application of panels, framing out of alignment, or improper fastening.

Joint Cracking. Appears either directly over the long edge or butt ends of boards, or may appear along the edge of taped joints. Often caused by structural movement and/or hygrometric and thermal expansion and contraction, or by excessively fast drying of joint compounds.

Field Cracking. Usually appears as diagonal crack originating from a corner of a partition or intersection with structural elements. Also seen directly over a structural element in center of a partition. May originate from corners of doors, light fixtures, and other weak areas in the surface created by penetration. Caused by structural movement described earlier in this chapter.

Angle Cracking. Appears directly in the apex of wall-ceiling or interior angles where partitions intersect. Also can appear as cracking at edge of paper reinforcing tape near surface intersections. Can be caused by structural movement or improper application of joint compound in corner angle.

Bead Cracking. Shows up along edge of flange. Caused by improper bead attachment, faulty bead, or joint compound application.

Wavy Surfaces. Boards are not flat but have a bowed or undulating surface. Caused by improper board fit, misaligned framing, hygrometric or thermal expansion.

Board Sag. Occurs in ceilings, usually under

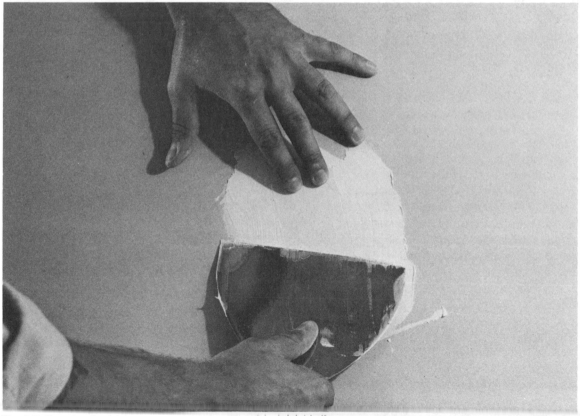

Fig. 6-6. Pressing the joint tape over the hole with a 6-inch joint knife.

Fig. 6-7. The completed patch, ready for sanding. The joint tape is completely hidden.

high-humidity conditions. Caused by insufficient framing support for board, board too thin for span, poor job conditions, improperly installed or mislocated vapor retarder, or improperly fitted panels.

Discoloration. Fractured, damaged or crushed boards after application may be caused by abuse or lumber shrinkage. Also see Discoloration below.

Discoloration. Board surface has slight difference in color over joints, supports or fasteners. Caused by improper paint finishing, uneven soiling and darkening from aging, or ultraviolet light.

Water Damage. Stains, paper bond failure, softness in board core or mildew growth are caused by sustained high humidity, standing water and improper protection from water leakage during transit and storage.

Checklist for Drywall Problems

To find the specific cause for a problem described above, check, on the following pages, all numerical references listed in the particular category.

fastener imperfections	3, 4, 5, 8, 9, 10, 11, 12, 22, 23, 24, 27
joint defects	1, 4, 6, 7, 14, 18, 19, 20, 21, 24, 25, 26, 27
loose panels	3, 4, 5, 7, 8, 9, 10, 11, 12, 22, 23
joint cracking	4, 7, 15, 16, 17, 21
field cracking	13
angle cracking	15, 17
bead cracking	15
wavy surfaces	3, 7, 16
board sag	7, 10, 28

surface defects	2, 13, 25, 26, 27
discoloration	24, 25, 26, 27
water damage	2

1. PANELS—Damaged Edges

Cause: Paper-bound edges have been damaged or abused; may result in ply separation along edge or in loosening of paper from gypsum core, or may fracture or powder the core itself. Damaged edges are more susceptible to ridging after joint treatment (Fig. 6-8).

Remedy: Cut back any severely damaged edges to sound board before application.

Prevention: Avoid using board with damaged edges that may easily be compressed, or can swell upon contact with moisture. Handle gypsum panels with reasonable care.

2. PANELS—Water-Damaged

Cause: During transit or storage, water has damaged panels; subject to scuffing, may develop paper bond failure. Dissolved glue from bundling tapes may damage board faces and cause them to stick together. If stored wet, may be subject to mildew. Prolonged soaking or exposure to water can soften core.

Remedy: Dry wet board completely before using;

handle board cautiously and re-pile with bundles separated by spacer strips of gypsum board. Check incoming board for water stains or dampness; protect carefully during shipment and storage. Do not erect damp panels, for this may result in paper bond failure. Replace boards having soft cores.

3. FRAMING—Members Out of Alignment

Cause: Due to misaligned top plate and stud (Fig. 6-9), hammering at points "X" as panels are applied on both sides of partition will probably result in nailheads puncturing paper or cracking board. Framing members more than ¼" out of alignment with adjacent members make it difficult to bring panels into firm contact with all nailing surfaces.

Remedy: Remove or drive in problem fasteners and only drive new fasteners into members in solid contact with board.

Prevention: Check alignment of studs, joists, headers, blocking and plates before applying panels, and correct before proceeding. Straighten badly bowed or crowned members. Shim out flush with adjoining surfaces. Use adhesive attachment.

4. FRAMING—Members Twisted

Cause: Framing members have not been properly squared with plates, presenting angular nailing surface (Fig. 6-10). When panels are applied, there is danger of puncturing paper with fastener heads or

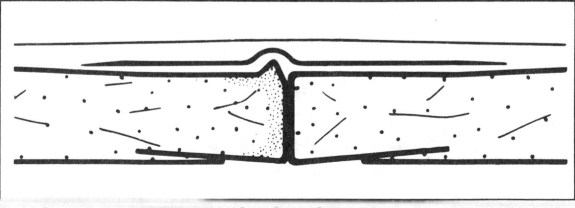

Fig. 6-8. Damaged edges (courtesy of the United States Gypsum Company).

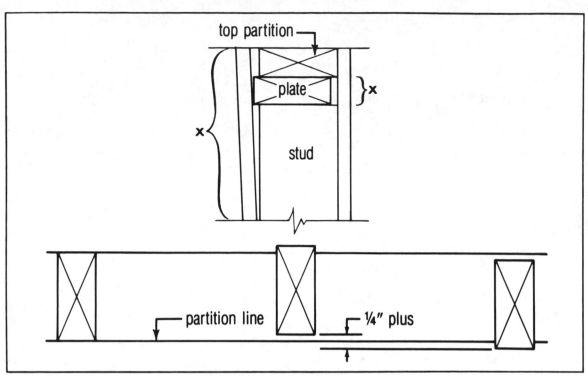

Fig. 6-9. Members out of alignment (courtesy of the United States Gypsum Company).

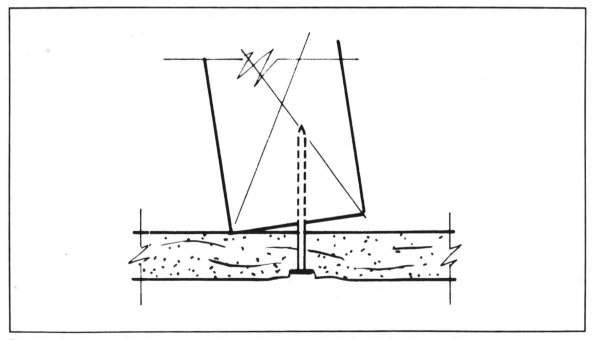

Fig. 6-10. Framing member is not square with plate (courtesy of the United States Gypsum Company).

of reverse twisting of member as it dries out, with consequent loosening of board and probable fastener pops. Warped or wet dimension lumber may contribute to deformity.

Remedy: After moisture content in framing has stabilized, remove problem fasteners and re-fasten with carefully driven USG Type W Screws.

Prevention: Align all twisted framing members before board application.

5. FRAMING—Protrusions

Cause: Bridging, headers, firestops, or mechanical lines have been installed improperly so as to project beyond face of framing, preventing panels from contacting nailing surface (Fig. 6-11). Result will be loose board, and fasteners driven in area of protrusion will probably puncture face paper.

Remedy and *Prevention:* Same as for FRAMING—Members Twisted.

6. FRAMING (Steel)—Panel Edges Out of Alignment

Cause: Improper placement of steel studs or advancing in wrong direction of panel installation can cause misalignment of panel edges and give the appearance of ridging when finished (Fig. 6-12).

Remedy: Fill and feather out joint with joint treatment.

Prevention: Install steel studs with all flanges pointed in the same direction. Then install panels by advancing in the direction opposite the flange direction.

7. PANELS—Improperly Fitted

Cause: Forcibly wedging an oversize panel into

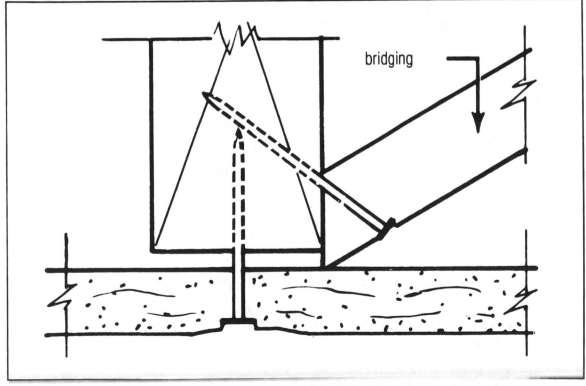

Fig. 6-11. Protrusion beyond the face of the framing (courtesy of the United States Gypsum Company).

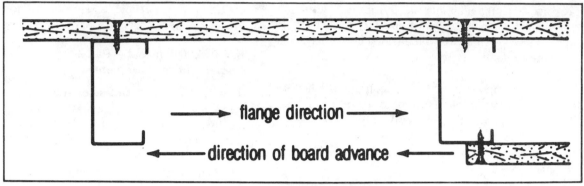

Fig. 6-12. Panel edges out of alignment (courtesy of the United States Gypsum Company).

place bows the panel and builds in stresses preventing it from contacting the framing (Fig. 6-13). Result: following fastening, a high percentage of fasteners on the central studs probably will puncture the paper. May also cause joint deformation.

Remedy: Remove panel, cut to fit properly, and replace. Fasten from center of panel toward ends and edges. Apply pressure to hold panel tightly against framing while driving fasteners.

8. FASTENERS—Puncturing of Face Paper

Cause: Poorly formed nailheads, careless nailing, excessively dry face paper or soft core. Nailheads which puncture paper and shatter core of panel (Fig. 6-14) have very little grip on board.

Remedy: Remove improperly driven fastener and properly drive new fastener.

Prevention: Correction of faulty framing (see

Framing Problems) and properly driven nails produce tight attachment with slight uniform dimple (Fig. 6-15). Nailhead bears on paper and holds panel securely against framing member. Use proper fastener or adhesive application. USG Screws with specially contoured head are best fastener known to eliminate cutting and fracturing. If face paper becomes dry and brittle, its low moisture content may aggravate nail cutting. Raise moisture content of board and humidity in work area.

9. FASTENERS—Nails Loosened by Pounding

Cause: Applying panels to the second side of a partition can loosen nails on opposite side. This is particularly true when lightweight, soft lumber, undersized studs or furring are used.

Remedy: Check panels for tightness on the partition side where panels were first applied. If looseness is detected, strike each nailhead an additional hammer blow, being careful to not overdrive the nail.

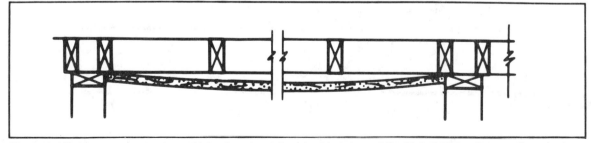

Fig. 6-13. Wedging an oversized panel into place bows the panel (courtesy of the United States Gypsum Company).

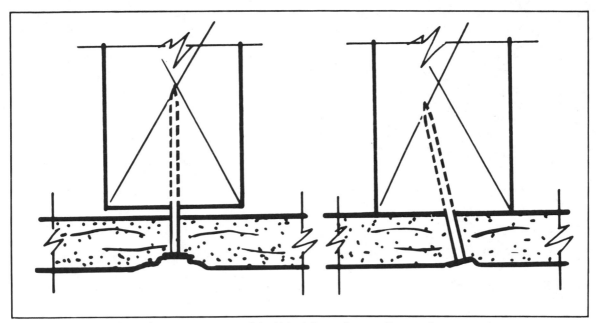

Fig. 6-14. Improperly driven fasteners (courtesy of the United States Gypsum Company).

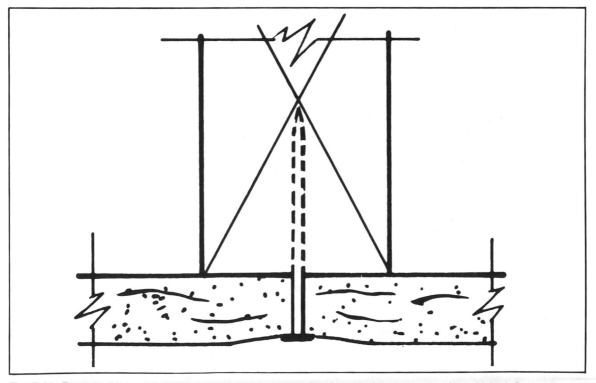

Fig. 6-15. Properly driven nail holds panel securely against framing member (courtesy of the United States Gypsum Company).

97

Prevention: Use proper framing, USG Type W Screws, or adhesive application.

10. FASTENERS—Unseated Nails

Cause: Flexible or extremely hard framing or furring does not permit nails to be properly driven. May result from undersized framing members, type of wood used or supports which exceed the maximum allowable frame spacing.

Remedy: Replace nails with 1¼″ USG Type W Screws.

Prevention: Use proper framing Type W Screws, or adhesive application.

11. FASTENERS—Loose Screws

Cause: Using the wrong type screw for the application or an improperly adjusted screwgun results in a screw stripping or not seating properly.

Remedy: Remove faulty fastener and replace with a properly driven screw.

Prevention: Use USG Screws with combination high/low threads for greater resistance to stripping and pullout; set screwgun clutch to proper depth.

12. PANELS—Loosely Fastened

Cause: Framing members are uneven because of misalignment or warping; lack of hand pressure on panel during fastening. Head of fastener alone cannot pull panel into firm contact with uneven members. Also see PANELS—Improperly Fitted.

Remedy: With nail attachment, during final blows of hammer apply additional pressure with hand to panel adjacent to nail (Fig. 6-16) to bring panel into contact with framing.

Prevention: Correct framing imperfections before

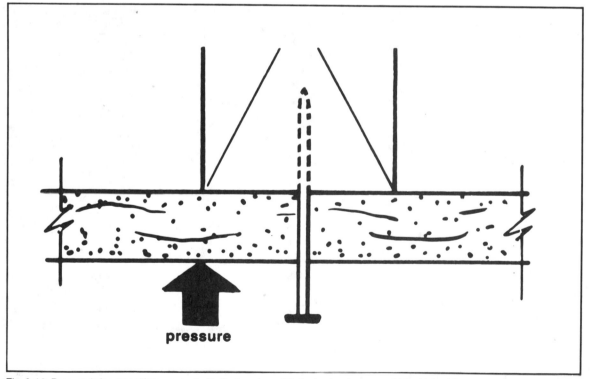

Fig. 6-16. Press to bring panel into contact with the framing while fastening (courtesy of the United States Gypsum Company).

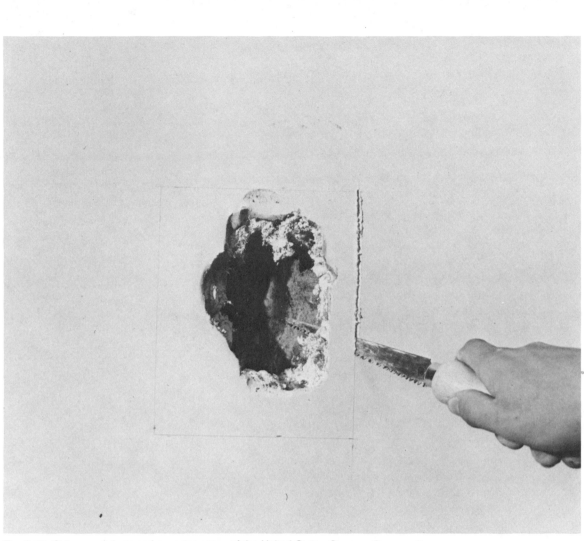

Fig. 6-17. Cut around damaged area (courtesy of the United States Gypsum Company).

applying panels; for a more solid attachment, use 1¼″ USG Type W Screws or use adhesive method.

13. PANELS—Surface Fractured After Application

a. *Cause:* Heavy blows or other abuse have fractured finished wall surface—too large a break for repair with joint compound.

Remedy: Cut a square-shaped or triangular section around damaged area, with a utility or keyhole saw (Fig. 6-17); use a rasp or sanding block to slope edges inward at 45°. Cut corresponding plug from sound gypsum panel, sand edges to exact fit (Fig. 6-18). If necessary, cement extra slat of gypsum panel to back of face layer to serve as brace. Butter edges (Fig. 6-19) and finish as a butt joint with joint compound (Fig. 6-20).

b. *Cause:* Attaching panel directly to flat grain of wide-dimensional wood framing members such as floor joists and headers. Shrinkage of wood causes fracture of board.

Remedy: As above, where appropriate, or repair as for joint ridging.

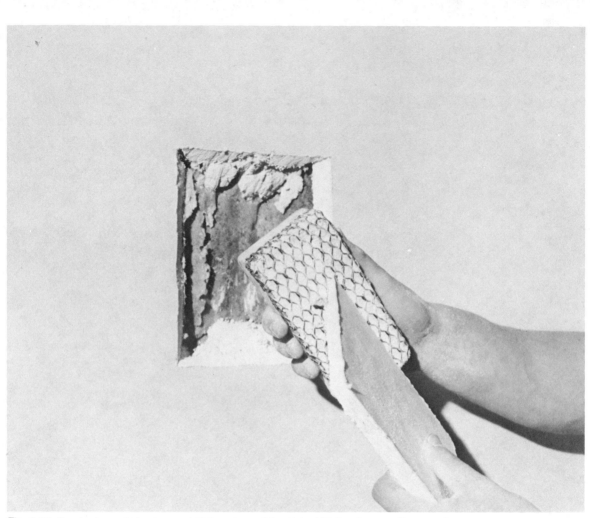

Fig. 6-18. Sand edges of plug to exact fit (courtesy of the United States Gypsum Company).

Prevention: To provide a flexible base to allow for movement of framing, attach RC-1 Resilient Channel to framing members and apply panels. Allow ½″ space at bottom edges of board for movement. Or attach board directly to studs but allow ¼″ separation between panels, and install USG Control Joint No. 093.

c. *Cause:* Knife scoring beyond corner of cutout for electrical boxes, light fixtures and door and window openings produces cracks in panel surface.

Remedy: Repair cuts with joint compound and tape before finishing.

Prevention: Stop score marks at corners, cut openings accurately.

d. *Cause:* Abnormal stress buildup resulting from structural deflection or racking discussed earlier in this chapter.

Remedy: Relieve stress, provide adequate isolation and retape, feathering joint compound over board area to disguise buildup.

Prevention: Provide proper isolation from structure to prevent stress buildup.

100

e. *Cause:* Excessive stresses resulting from hygrometric and/or thermal expansion and contraction discussed earlier in this chapter.

Remedy: Correct unsatisfactory environmental conditions, provide sufficient relief and retape, feathering joint compound over broad area.

Prevention: Correct improper job conditions and install control joints for relief in long partition runs and large ceiling areas.

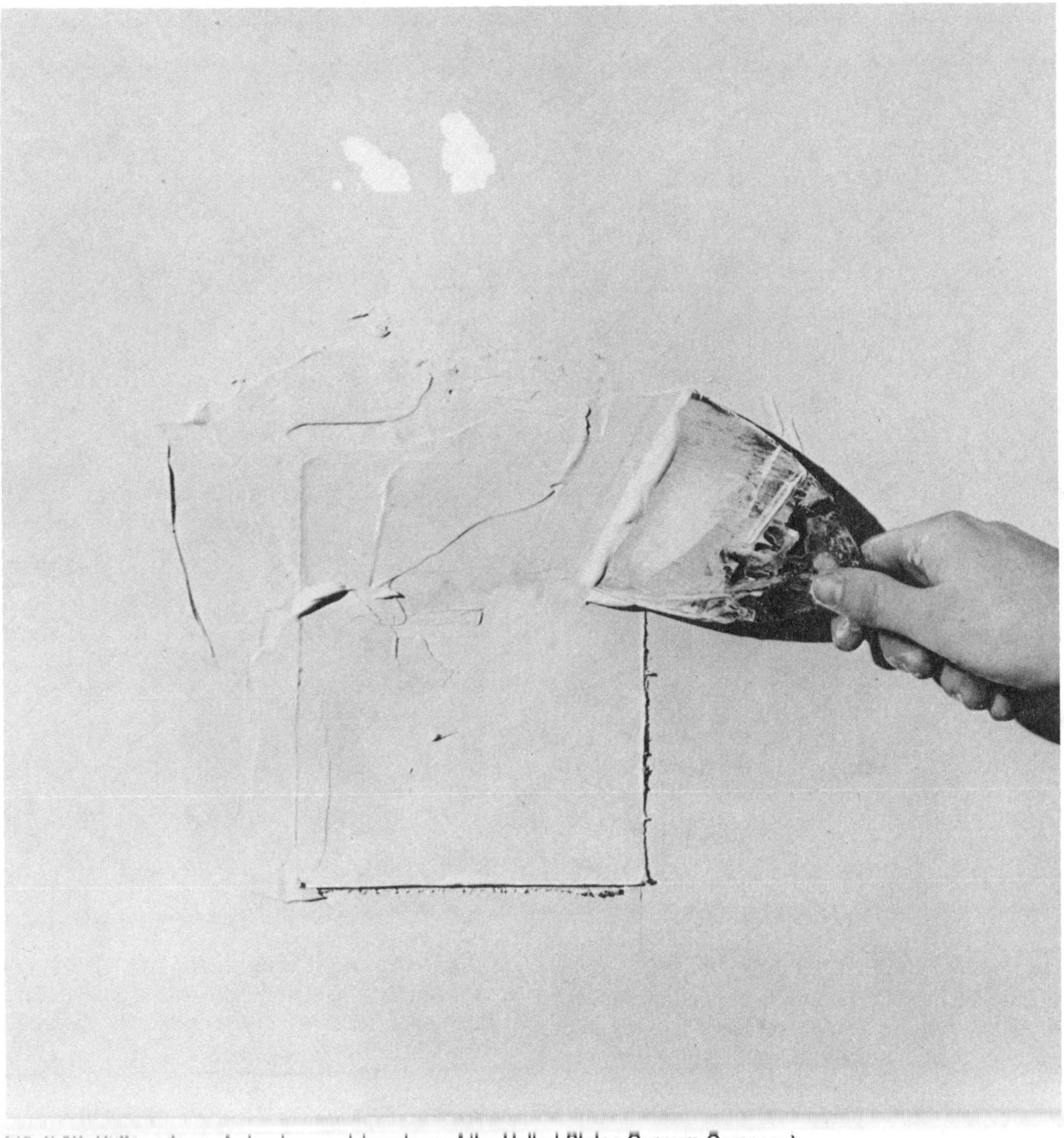

Fig. 6-19. Butter edges of plug to panel (courtesy of the United States Gypsum Company).

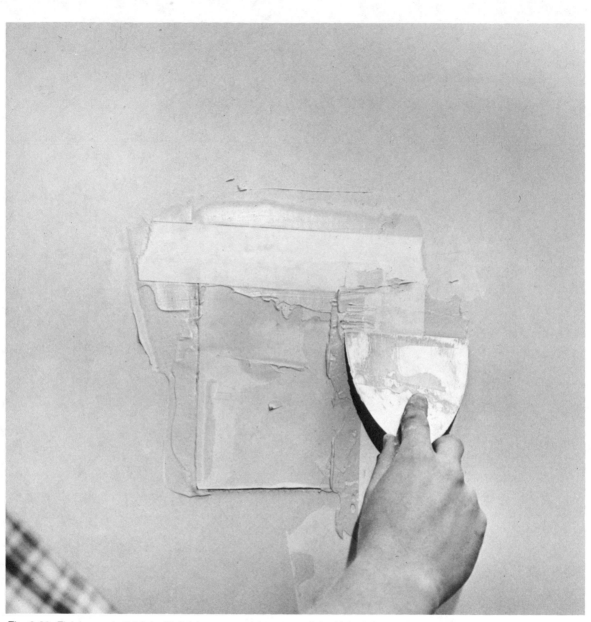

Fig. 6-20. Finish as a butt joint with joint compound (courtesy of the United States Gypsum Company).

14. JOINTS—Blisters in Tape

Cause: Insufficient or overly thin compound was used under the tape, or tape was not initially pressed into good contact with the compound; or too much compound was forced from under tape by application of excessive tool pressure when embedding.

Remedy: Open up blistered area by slitting tape. Fill cut with joint compound and press tape back in place with knife blade. When dry smooth to level finish.

Prevention: Provide sufficient compound under entire tape.

15. JOINTS—Edge Cracking

a. *Cause:* After joint treatment, straight narrow cracks along edges of tape result from: too rapid drying because of high temperature accompanied by low humidity, or excessive drafts; improper application, such as overdilution of joint compound, use of wrong compound (topping instead of taping), excessive joint compound under tape or failure to follow embedding with a skim coat over tape; cold, wet application conditions which also may cause poor bond.

Because this problem is difficult to see when it first occurs, it may not be discovered until decoration begins. However, the cause can be attributed to some aspect of the taping operation.

Remedy: Especially when poor atmospheric conditions exist, carefully examine all joints after taping and skimming applications have dried; repairs are more economical at this stage. Cut away any weakly bonded tape edges. Fill hairline cracks with cut shellac (2 to 3 lb.); groove out larger cracks with sharp tool, coat with shellac and allow to dry, then refill with joint compound; or cover cracks with complete joint treatment including reinforcing tape, feather to surface level with plane of board.

Prevention: Use either USG Ready-Mixed Joint Compound or DURABOND Joint Compound which have best built-in resistance to cracks; place shielding devices over room openings to prevent drafts; do not apply joint treatment over hot surfaces; wet down floors if room humidity is too low; during cold weather, control heat at min. 55° F (13° C) and supply good ventilation. Avoid practices listed under *"Cause."*

b. *Cause:* After joint treatment, cracks along edges of corner bead or trim can result from the same unsatisfactory conditons listed above for tape. Also can be caused by impact on the bead.

Remedy: Remove applied joint compound, securely fasten corner bead or trim to framing beneath panels, refinish bead with joint compound.

Prevention: Use USG 800 Series Corner Bead and

Trim with expanded flanges which minimize cracking.

16. JOINTS—Center Cracking

a. *Cause:* Abnormal stress buildup resulting from structural deflection or racking discussed earlier in this chapter.

Remedy: Relieve stress, provide adequate isolation and retape, feathering joint compound over broad area to disguise buildup.

Prevention: Provide proper isolation from structure to prevent stress buildup.

b. *Cause:* Excessive stresses resulting from hygrometric and/or thermal expansion and contraction discussed earlier in this chapter.

Remedy: Correct unsatisfactory environment conditions, provide sufficient relief and retape, feathering joint compound over broad area.

Prevention: Correct improper job conditions and install control joints for relief in long partition runs and large ceiling areas.

17. JOINTS—Angle Cracking

a. *Cause:* Too much compound applied over tape at apex of angle.

Remedy: After compound is completely dry, smooth out excess compound at apex; fill only hairline cracks with compound. Do not apply additional compound which will build up.

Prevention: Keep excess compound from corner, leaving only a small amount or no compound in apex.

b. *Cause:* Slitting or scoring reinforcing tape during application. May result from use of improper tool.

Remedy: If crack extends through the tape, retape and finish.

Prevention: Use proper tool for corner treatment.
c. *Cause:* Structural or thermal movement resulting from two dissimilar materials or constructions.

Remedy: Remove tape, provide relief, finish with angle edge trim and caulk.

Prevention: Use channel-type or angle edge trim over gypsum board where two dissimilar surfaces interface.

18. JOINTS—High Crowns

Cause: Excessive piling of compound over joint; compound not feathered out beyond shoulders, improper bedding of tape; framing out of alignment or panel edges not tight against framing; improper adjustment of tools; misuse of or worn tools.

Remedy: Sand joints to flush surface (take care to avoid scuffing paper by oversanding).

Prevention: Embed tape properly, using only enough compound to cover tape and fill taper depression, or tape itself at butt joints; feather compound far enough to conceal.

19. JOINTS—Excessive and/or Delayed Shrinkage

Cause: (1) Atmospheric conditions—slow drying and high humidity; (2) Insufficient drying time between coats of compound; (3) Excessive water added in mixing compound; (4) Heavy fills.

Remedy: See Starved Joints.

20. JOINTS—Starved Joints

Cause: This is a form of delayed shrinkage caused chiefly by insufficient drying time between coats of compound. May also be caused by insufficient compound applied over tape to fill taper, overthinning or oversmoothing of compound. Shrinkage usually progresses until drying is complete.

Remedy: Use fast-hardening DURABOND 45, 90, 150, 210 or 300 Joint Compound or reapply a full cover coat of heavy-mixed compound over tape—

since this is heaviest application, most shrinkage will take place in this coat, making it easier to fill taper properly. Finish by standard procedure.

Prevention: Allow each coat of joint compound to dry thoroughly before applying succeeding coat, or use a low-shrinkage DURABOND Compound.

21. JOINTS—Ridging

Causes: All building materials grow or shrink in response to changes in temperature and humidity. When they are confined to a specific space, such as gypsum panels in a partition or ceiling, they are put under stress, either compression or tension, depending on the temperature or humidity conditions. These stresses are relieved when the panel bends outward in the region of the joint. Once this bending takes place, the system takes a set and never returns to normal. It becomes progressively worse with each change of temperature or humidity. This progressive deformation appears as a continuous ridge along length of joint, with uniform fine, ridge-like pattern at center.

Remedy: (1) Let ridge develop fully before undertaking repairs—usually six months is sufficient. Make repairs under hot and dry conditions; (2) Smooth ridge down to reinforcing tape without cutting through tape. Fill concave areas on either side of ridge with light fill of thick-mix compound. After this is dry, float very thin film of compound over entire area; (3) Examine area with strong sidelighting to make certain that ridge has been concealed. If not, use additional feathering coats of compound. Redecorate. Ridging can recur, but if it does it is usually less severe. Continuous wetting will aggravate conditon.

Prevention: Use Sheetrock Brand SW Panels with the exclusive rounded edge designed to prevent ridging. Follow general recommendations for joint treatment and approved application procedure, which includes back-blocking and laminated double-layer application to minimize potential ridging problems. Pay particular attention to temperature, ventilation, consistency of compound, prompt covering coat over tape, minimum width of fill, finish coats and required drying time between coats.

22. FASTENERS—Nail Pops from Lumber Shrinkage

Cause: Improper application, lumber shrinkage or a combination of both. With panels held reasonably tight against framing member and with proper-length nails, only severe shrinkage of the lumber normally will cause nail pops. But if nailed loosely, any inward pressure on panel will push nailhead through its thin covering pad of compound. Pops resulting from "nail creep" occur when shrinkage of the wood framing exposes nail shank and consequently loosens panel (see Lumber Shrinkage).

Remedy: Repairs usually are necessary only for pops which protrude .005″ or more from face of board (Fig. 6-21). Smaller protrusions may require repair if they occur in a smooth gloss surface or flat-painted surface under extreme lighting conditions. Those which appear before or during decora-

tion should be repaired immediately. Pops which occur after one month's heating or more are usually caused wholly or partly by wood shrinkage, and should not be repaired until near end of heating season. An often effective procedure for resetting a popped nail is to place a 4″ broad knife over the nail and hit with hammer to seat flush with surface. A more permanent method is to drive proper nail or USG Type W Screw about 1½″ from popped nail while applying sufficient pressure adjacent to nailhead to bring panel in firm contact with framing. Strike popped nail lightly to seat it below surface of board. Remove loose compound, apply finish coats of compound and paint.

Prevention: Proper nail application; use of lumber meeting Framing Requirements; attachment with USG Type W Screws or by adhesive application.

23. FASTENERS—Bulge Around Fastener

Cause: Overdriving fasteners, driving them with the wrong tool or failing to hold board firmly against framing while driving fasteners can puncture and

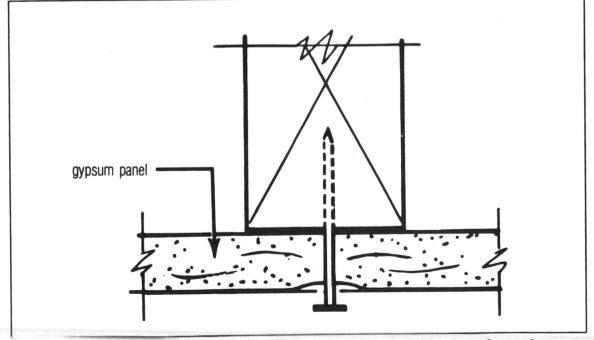

Fig. 6-21. Repair nail pops which protrude more than .005″ or more (courtesy of the United States Gypsum Company).

bulge face paper and damage core of board. Following application of joint compound or texture finish that wets the board paper can result in board bulging or swelling around fastener.

Remedy: Drive screw fastener close to damaged area, clean out damaged paper core, repair with DURABOND Joint Compound and refinish.

Prevention: Use correct tool and drive fasteners properly. Also see Panels—Loosely Fastened.

24. FINISH—Discoloration

Cause: Differences in suction of panel paper and joint compound may lighten paint color or change gloss or sheen in higher-suction areas; most common when conventional oil paints are used; also caused by overthinning of paint. May also occur over fasteners in ceilings subjected to severe artificial or natural side lighting. Suction differences may also cause greater amounts of texturing material to be deposited over high-suction areas, causing color differences when viewed from an angle. Before painting, face panel paper may be darkened from exposure to sunlight.

Remedy: Redecorate. *Prevention:* Before painting or texturing, seal surface properly with a good quality white alkyd flat wall paint, latex or solvent base primer sealer. Take care to avoid roughening surface paper, when sanding joint compound.

25. FINISH—Gloss
Variation with High Gloss Paints

Cause: Differences in suction of panel paper and joint compound (as stated in no. 24, above). Problem is accentuated by strong side lighting with slight angle of incidence to ceiling or wall surface.

Remedy: Redecorate. *Prevention:* Before painting with a high gloss paint, apply a skim coat of joint compound over the entire wall surface or use a veneer plaster system.

26. FINISH—Joint Darkening

Cause: This condition occurs most commonly with color tinted paint rather than white. Most severe when applied in humid weather or when joints have not fully dried; also when high or medium-alkaline joint compounds have been used.

Remedy: Apply a good quality white alkyd flat wall paint, latex or solvent base primer sealer. Repaint only after joints are thoroughly dry.

Prevention: Be sure joints are thoroughly dry before painting.

27. FINISH—Shadowing

Cause: Temperature differential in outside walls or top-floor ceilings causes collection of airborne dust on colder spots of interior surface, resulting in photographing or shadowing over fasteners, furring or framing. Most severe with great indoor-outdoor temperature variation.

Remedy: Wash painted surfaces, remove spots with wallpaper cleaner, or redecorated surfaces; change air filters regularly.

Prevention: Use double-layer application with adhesively applied face layer. Use separately framed free-standing interior wall surface and insulate in void to reduce temperature difference between steel or wood components and panels.

28. PANELS—Board Sag

a. *Cause:* Too much weight from overlaid insulation; exposure to sustained high humidity; vapor retarder improperly installed or wetting causes ceiling panels to sag after installation. Also caused by installing board too thin for framing spacing.

Remedy: Remove sagged board or fur ceiling using RC-1 Resilient Channels and apply another layer of board.

Prevention: See Chapter 3 for proper frame spacing and application procedures.

b. *Cause:* Water-based textures wet face paper and weaken gypsum core, causing ceiling panels to sag after installation.

Remedy: Same as 28a. *Prevention:* See Chapter 3 for proper frame spacing and application procedures.

Chapter 7

Mounting Fixtures

Most everyone has experienced the frustration of attempting to attach something to a gypsum wall or ceiling, only to have the nails or screws pull loose from the wallboard. Decorative and functional items can be installed on drywall without fear of them coming loose and falling. It is not even necessary to fasten them to studs or joists.

Fixtures of substantial weight can be hung on drywall using either spring-loaded toggle bolts or expanding wall anchors. Figure 7-1 shows several types and sizes of each, they come in many types and sizes. Spring-loaded toggle bolts should be used to support extremely heavy items or fixtures such as shelves that will support a great deal of weight. The size of the toggle bolt required is determined by the amount of weight it must support. Toggle bolt size is indicated by the nominal size of the bolt that screws into the spring-loaded wing assembly (such as ¼ inch).

Expanding wall anchors can be used in applications where the size and holding power of a spring-loaded toggle bolt is not required. Expanding wall anchors should be used in place of toggle bolts wherever possible. Once a spring-loaded toggle bolt is installed, it is somewhat permanent. The bolt can easily be removed, but the toggle assembly will be lost once the bolt is taken out. With an expanding wall anchor, the screw can be removed, but the anchor itself remains in place—allowing easy replacement of the screw.

The size of an expanding wall anchor is usually indicated by three dimensions; the length of the shaft after expansion, the diameter of the hole required, and the thread size of the screw. An example would be ½″ × ⅜″ × 6-32. Such a wall anchor would be used for mounting in ½-inch wallboard. It would require a ⅜-inch mounting hole and would accommodate a #6-32 (#6 American wire gauge, 32 threads per inch) machine screw. The size of expanding wall anchor required is determined primarily by wallboard thickness (which is the same as expanded length). The other dimensions of the

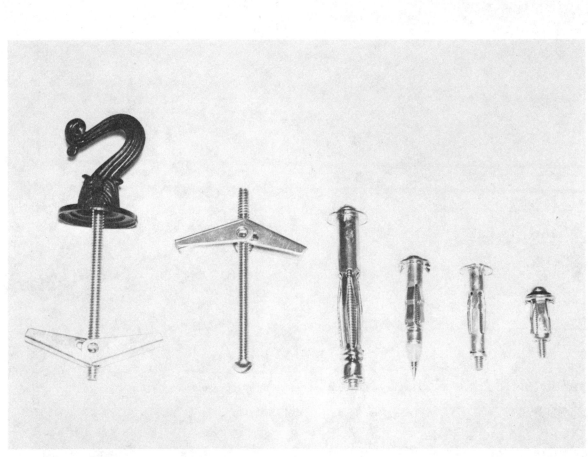

Fig. 7-1. An assortment of toggle bolts and wall anchors.

wall anchor will be proportional to the length.

INSTALLING
SPRING-LOADED TOGGLE BOLTS

Installing a spring-loaded toggle bolt in drywall is a simple task. First, carefully mark the position of the bolt on the wallboard. Next, drill a hole in the wallboard just big enough to slip the folded wing assembly through. The hole should be drilled (not punched). The impact of driving a punch will fracture the wallboard on the back, reducing the strength of the wallboard and the completed toggle bolt installation. If you find yourself drilling into a stud or joist, use a wood screw or lag bolt (a very big wood screw) instead.

After the hole is drilled, fold the spring-loaded wings of the toggle assembly back and insert the

entire bolt assembly through the hole as shown in Fig. 7-2. Once the wings clear the hole they will expand. Pull out on the bolt so the wings are held against the back of the wallboard and tighten the bolt. When the bolt is fully tightened, the wings will flatten out against the back of the wallboard, as in Fig. 7-3, providing a very sturdy anchor.

INSTALLING EXPANDING WALL ANCHORS

Installing expanding wall anchors in drywall is as easy as installing spring-loaded toggle bolts. Some expanding wall anchors require that a hole be drilled first. Others are sharp on the end and can be driven into the wallboard like a nail. I recommend that a hole be drilled for either type to avoid fracturing the wallboard in the back.

To install an expanding wall anchor, start by

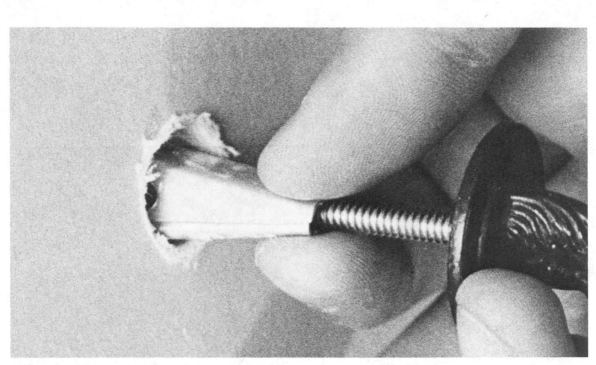

Fig. 7-2. Installing a spring-loaded toggle bolt through a predrilled hole in gypsum wallboard.

Fig. 7-3. Back side of an installed spring-loaded toggle bolt.

drilling a hole no larger than the diameter of the anchor shank. Next, slip the anchor into the hole and push it firmly against the wallboard surface. Most expanding wall anchors have at least two teeth on the flange that sink into the wallboard and prevent it from rotating during expansion. Make sure these teeth penetrate the wallboard. Some expanding wall anchors also come with a small wrench that is used to hold them fast during expansion and tightening. Such a wall anchor is shown being tightened in Fig. 7-4.

After the anchor is seated, the shank must be expanded. This is done by tightening the screw completely. As the screw pulls on the shank, the sections are expanded against the back of the wallboard (as in Fig. 7-5). Once the anchor shaft is expanded, the screw can be removed (and the in-

tended fixture fastened with it). Be sure the wall anchor is mounted securely before mounting anything on it.

FINDING STUDS AND JOISTS

Sometimes it is necessary to find the studs or joists in a finished drywall system. Before the wallboards were hung, the positions of the studs should have been marked on the subfloor and underlayment. If you have access to these marks, finding the studs will be easy. If you don't, you will have to use one of the methods described below to find them.

The oldest method of finding studs and joists is to "tap them out" using a hammer and a piece of cardboard. See Fig. 7-6. Tap the wallboard surface and listen to the sound of the tapping. Move across the wall or ceiling as you tap. The wall cavity will

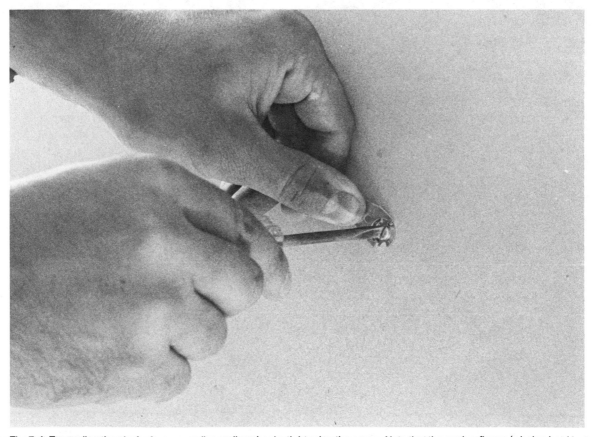

Fig. 7-4. Expanding the shaft of an expanding wall anchor by tightening the screw. Note that the anchor flange is being held fast with a special wrench that came with the anchor.

111

Fig. 7-5. Back side view of an installed expanding wall anchor.

sound hollow between framing members and solid as you approach studs or joists.

Once you think you have found a stud or joist, mark the spot and drive a nail into the wallboard to see if you strike wood. If you don't drive into something solid, try it again an inch in either direction until you do hit wood. Mark the spot prominently and then patch up the other holes you made in your wallboard. Wallboard repairs are covered in Chapter 6. Tapping out studs is best done as close to the floor as possible on walls, and as close as possible to a wall on ceilings. This way the patched holes won't be too obvious.

It is best to find each stud or joist individually. The studs in a wall can be spaced at 16 or 24 inches on center. The joists in a ceiling could be 12, 16, or 24 inches apart. Don't assume that studs are always on 16-inch centers. Find at least two and be sure. Also consider that ceiling joists can run in either direction. Normally they will span the shorter dimension of a room.

An alternate method of finding studs and joists is to use a magentic studfinder. A magnetic studfin-der actually finds the nails in a stud or joist. In Fig. 7-7, a magnetic studfinder is shown being used to locate a wall stud. To use such a device, you'll have to make a guess at where the nails are. On most walls, they should be between 8 and 12 inches up from the floor and the same distance from the walls on a ceiling. Once the studfinder hits a nail, the needle will point to it like a compass needle points north.

The easiest and most reliable method of finding studs and joists is to use an electronic studfinder like the one shown in Fig. 7-8. The lights on the front of the device light up one at a time as you approach a wall stud or ceiling joist. Once you are over a framing member, they all light. The device finds the actual stud or joist—not the nails. It can be used on any wall surface of any thickness. My electronic studfinder has never been wrong yet.

The mounting of some items on drywall will require knowledge of how the wall or ceiling is built. The Appendix contains diagrams of standard framing methods showing some of the pertinent details of wall and ceiling construction.

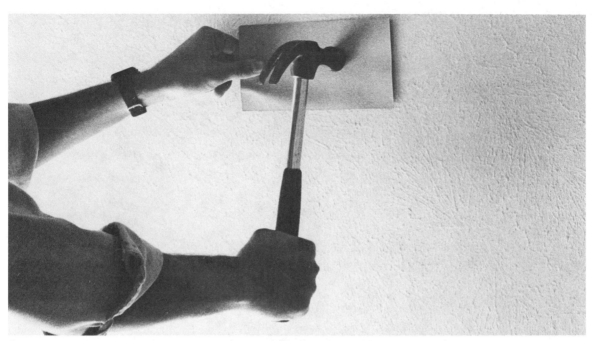

Fig. 7-6. Tapping out the wall studs with a hammer and a piece of cardboard. The cardboard is used to protect the wallboard surface.

Fig. 7-7. Using a magnetic studfinder to locate a wall stud. The needle of the device is pointing to a nailhead.

113

Fig. 7-8. Using an electronic studfinder is the easiest and most foolproof method of locating wall studs and ceiling joists (courtesy of Zircon International Inc.).

Chapter 8

Textured Ceilings

Besides adding depth and character to a room, ceiling textures can be used to disguise minor flaws and irregularities in ceilings. All the texture in the world won't hide major structural defects, but minor discrepancies can usually be hidden or made less obvious by applying ceiling texture.

TEXTURING MATERIALS

There are many types of texturing products available. Some come in powdered form and others come premixed, ready to apply. Many different surface types are available; they range from quite coarse to very subtle. Aggregate materials, such as glitter, mica chips, or silica sand, can be mixed into a texture to create a surface that sparkles when struck by light. Some ceiling textures can be tinted with paint, and many can be painted after they dry. Most can also be thinned with water to vary the courseness of their surface. Figure 8-1 shows just a few examples of the many ceiling textures on the market today.

One of the most popular and economical ceiling textures used by do-it-yourselfers is ordinary drywall joint compound. The same mud you finish your joints with also makes a good texturing material. The best type of mud to use for texturing a ceiling is premixed topping or all-purpose compound. Taping compound should not be used as a ceiling texture. It will undergo too much shrinkage during drying and, because it must be applied rather heavily for texturing, it will probably crack.

Mud used as a texture can be thinned with water to create various surface effects. Aggregate materials can easily be added to it. In some cases, you might be able to mix paint into the mud, but it is best to paint it after it has been applied and allowed to dry. Drywall joint compound is a very versatile material. When using it as a texture you are limited only by your imagination.

TEXTURING TOOLS

There must be hundreds of ways to create different patterns in a texture using various tools. Long-napped paint rollers, brushes, trowels, and serrated

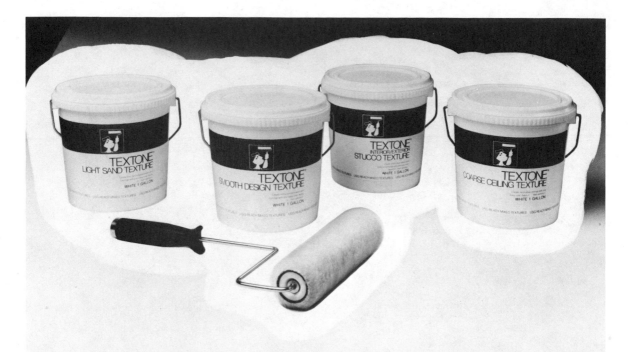

Fig. 8-1. Several ready-mixed ceiling textures with various surface types (courtesy of the United States Gypsum Company).

Fig. 8-2. A few of the many household items which can be used to create a ceiling texture with drywall joint compound.

116

glue spreaders are a few examples. Figure 8-2 shows a few items I found lying about that could be used to texture a ceiling.

A texture that was created with a long-napped paint roller is shown in Fig. 8-3. The coarseness of such a texture will depend on the nap length of the roller you use and the thickness of the mud. A longer nap will produce heavier depressions and greater shadowing in the surface of the mud (as will thicker mud). A stippled texture is shown in Fig. 8-4. A stippled surface is created with a brush. The one shown in Fig. 8-4 was made by blotting the mud with a round texturing brush. Similar patterns can be created using most any type of brush. Figure 8-5 shows a texture that was sprayed on. Most texturing materials, including mud, can be thinned sufficiently with water for spray-gun application.

Another popular pattern type is one that is troweled. After the mud is applied to the wallboard surface, it can be troweled to resemble stucco or scored to appear as rough masonry or block. Figures 8-6 and 8-7 show two types of tools that can be used to create such effects in a texture. Figure 8-6 shows a notched trowel. The notches on the side of the blade and those on the end can both be used to create different texture patterns. Such a trowel may come with round, pointed, or square notches in the blade, space any where from 1/16 to

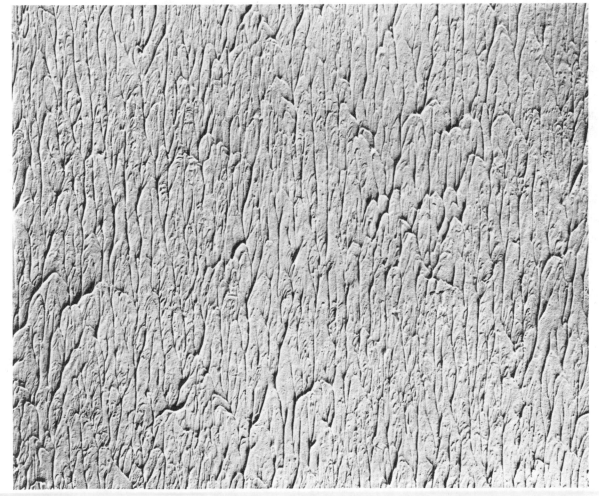

Fig. 8-8. A heavy texture pattern created with a long-napped paint roller (courtesy of the United States Gypsum Company).

117

Fig. 8-4. A stippled texture pattern created with a round brush (courtesy of the United States Gypsum Company).

¼ inch apart. The tool shown in Fig. 8-7 is a 9-inch glue spreader; it makes an excellent texturing tool.

The wall shown in Fig. 8-8 was textured using a similar tool. The pattern on the wall was applied in a

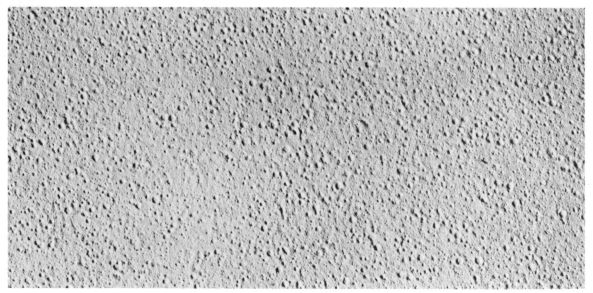

Fig. 8-5. A sprayed-on ceiling texture (courtesy of the United States Gypsum Company).

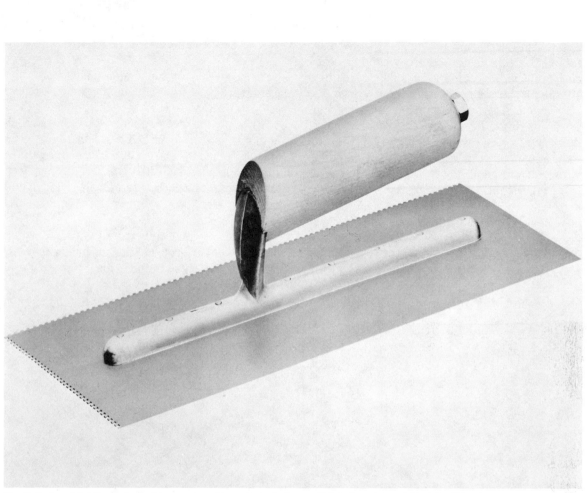

Fig. 8-6. A notched trowel used to create patterns in texturing materials (courtesy of Red Devil Inc.).

random manner, yet there is still a definite pattern to it. The strokes of the blade were almost all made horizontally or vertically at random length with only a few at an angle.

BEFORE YOU START

Many a beginning drywaller has applied joint compound as a ceiling texture, because he heard he didn't have to finish his joints or paint his ceiling first, only to find out he heard wrong. A certain amount of surface preparation is necessary prior to applying a mud texture or any type of texture for that matter.

Before a gypsum wallboard ceiling can be textured, the nailheads and joints must receive a filler coat and should be given a second coat of joint compound as described in Chapter 5. The application of a finish coat is not necessary.

You might be able to apply texture to bare drywall without any problems, but you should either prime or paint the wallboard with a decent alkyd or latex-based primer or flat wall paint first. Doing so will ensure uniform absorption across the wallboard and the joints and reduce the chance of the joints showing through the texture.

If you are texturing over old paint, be sure to wash the surface thoroughly first. Remove all dust and dirt with a mild detergent. Nicotine stains can remain because they won't affect the bonding or color of the finished texture. Mold and mildew must be removed. To remove mold or mildew, scrub the surface with a solution of 1 part bleach to 3 parts water. After scrubbing the stain with the bleach solution, wipe it clean and apply another coat of bleach, allowing it to air dry. This should effectively kill the fungus and prevent it from returning.

It wouldn't hurt to spot paint the stain before texturing either. Be very careful with the bleach. Wear safety goggles when using it. This is especially important when you use bleach on the ceiling. Water stains should also be spot painted before texturing and the cause of the stain should be corrected.

Before texturing, fill, tape, and finish any cracks in the wallboard or joints. Fixing them before you texture will be much easier than fixing them once the texture is cracked too.

APPLYING THE TEXTURE

The best method of applying a mud texture (and most others) is to trowel it onto the wallboard first and texture it after it is applied. Beginning in a corner, apply the mud to the drywall with a 12-inch joint knife. Cover about half a wallboard (16 to 24 square feet) and then go back and create the pattern in it. Simply continue this two-step process until you are done. The entire texturing job need not be done all at once. You can spread it out over several weekends if you like.

If you are going to texture the ceiling with a roller, you might be able to thin the mud with water and roll it directly onto the ceiling, texturing it at

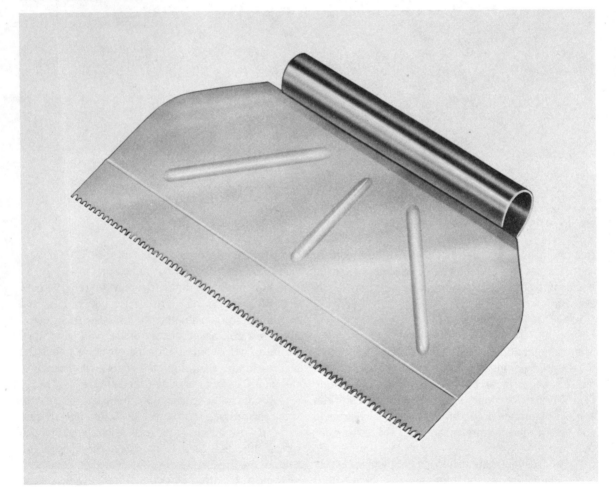

Fig. 8-7. A 9-inch glue spreader which can be used to produce attractive patterns in ceiling textures (courtesy of Red Devil Inc.).

Fig. 8-8. A very heavy texture applied and created with a notched trowel (courtesy of the United States Gypsum Company).

the same time and saving yourself some work. It's a good idea to practice on a piece of scrap before you actually do the ceiling. Once the texture is up, you will pretty much have to live with it. When you are texturing the ceiling, stop and admire your work often. That way, if you don't like the result, you can make corrections before the texture material dries.

The coverage you will get from a bucket of mud will vary based on the thickness of the coat you apply and the consistency of the texture material. Most texture materials have coverage data on the packages. A 5-gallon bucket of mud will cover about 32 square feet, or one full 8-foot wallboard if applied ¼ inch thick. That is a very heavy coat though. At

half that thickness you can double the coverage. If you thin the mud with water and roll it directly onto the ceiling, you can expect to cover about 300 square feet with a 5-gallon bucket.

Be sure you can use the same brand of texture or mud throughout the entire texturing job. The color and consistency of muds and textures will vary between manufacturers. It is also not advisable to mix compounds made by different companies or even different compounds made by the same company. Many times they will contain additives or agents that are incompatible.

A finished texture can be painted after it dries. Allow a full three days drying time before painting a fresh texture and more if it was applied heavily. Although the surface may appear dry, it will still be damp underneath. Use a long-napped roller to apply the paint.

It is usually not advisable to texture walls. This is especially true if there are children in the house. A textured wall can be very hard to maintain. If you do decide to texture a wall, use a hardening type of compound like those discussed in Chapter 2.

Some hardening compounds cure as hard as concrete. For texture application, select a hardening compound that provides a 45- to 60-minute curing time. This will give you enough time to apply it and pattern it before it hardens.

A properly applied ceiling texture will enhance the beauty of your home and give you years of satisfactory service with little or no maintenance.

Chapter 9

Building Codes, Permits, and Inspections

Almost any construction you perform, whether new construction or alteration to an existing structure, is covered under one of the nationally recognized model codes. Some of the codes are:

The Uniform Building Code
The One & Two Family Dwelling Code
The Uniform Mechanical Code
The Uniform Plumbing Code
The National Electrical Code

There are other codes in addition to these. The ones listed above are the most important. Almost any project a do-it-yourselfer undertakes will be covered in detail by some or all of the building codes discussed in this chapter.

The building codes are written by building officials in collaboration with professionals such as engineers, manufacturers, fire scientists, and insurance underwriters. The codes are written to ensure your safety, health, and protection.

You should be able to obtain more information about the building codes from your local building department. Undoubtedly they maintain copies of their own and possibly copies for sale to the general public.

BUILDING CODES

Building codes cover the basic structural requirements for habitable buildings and structures intended for occupancy and assembly by people. Of particular concern to the homeowner or do-it-yourselfer is the *One & Two Family Dwelling Code.* The information contained in it is extracted from the *Uniform Building Code,* which is much broader in scope and content. The *Uniform Building Code* contains engineering data that is extremely useful to architects and contractors.

The *One & Two Family Dwelling Code* contains, in table form, such items as stud and joist size versus span, nail size and spacing, foundation width and depth, and wall-covering attachments (including gypsum wallboard).

PLUMBING CODE

The Uniform Plumbing Code specifies what can and

cannot be done with the water and sewage pipes in your home. The plumbing code provides specifications on products, materials, and installation methods. Sinks, showers, dishwashers, toilets, hot-water heaters, and similar fixtures are all covered under this code.

MECHANICAL CODE

The Uniform Mechanical Code covers the standards and methods of installation pertaining to the mechanical fixtures in your home. Mechanical fixtures include such things as heating, cooling, air conditioning, and ventilation devices. The size, type, and installation of the ductwork associated with these devices is also covered in the mechanical code.

THE NATIONAL ELECTRICAL CODE

The National Electrical Code specifies what can and cannot be done with the wiring inside and outside your home. This code covers such things as product and material standards, minimum wire gauges, circuit breaker and fuse ratings, and wiring and fixture installations.

This is an extremely important code. The consequences of improper installation or selection of materials are severe. The electrical code must be followed to the letter when installing electrical wiring and fixtures.

BUILDING PERMITS

It is essential that you take out a building permit for any construction you perform other than minor repairs or improvements to your home. There are several reasons I say this.

The purchase of a building permit has many advantages. First, a building permit entitles you to the services of a building inspector. There is no substitute for his expertise and advice. When you purchase the permit, you also purchase his professional services.

Second, a building permit legally protects you. Many times a zoning permit must be obtained prior to the issue of a building permit. A perfect example would be the addition or extension of a garage to your home. In applying for a zoning permit, you would most likely be required to provide a floor plan showing the distances of the proposed structure from the street and your property lines. The zoning department would review the drawing to ensure that you remain within your legal limits and do not encroach on any easement or right-of-way.

Third, your safety would be ensured. All of your work would be subjected to building inspections. They would have to comply with the standards set forth in the applicable codes.

Last but not least, you are financially protected by a building permit. If you should finish your basement without obtaining a permit, your work would never be inspected. Suppose a fire starts in your garage, and the house burns to the ground. The fact that you performed illegal construction becomes a very convenient excuse for your insurance company not to pay off on the damages. You can rest assured that they will use it as an excuse even though the room you altered did not cause the fire.

Applying for a building permit is a simple process. You do not need to be a licensed contractor of any type to obtain a building permit, providing you own the structure on which you are working. The fee is usually around $15 or $20 for most home improvement projects. For some things, a sketch or plan will have to be provided with the permit application. For most projects, however, a simple description of the work on the application itself will do. Figure 9-1 shows a typical building permit application form.

Figure 9-2 shows a typical building permit. Some locales require that the permit be prominently posted at the construction site. Even if yours does not, it is a good idea to do so.

The individual who is actually issued the building permit is responsible for the correctness and the completion of the work for which the permit was issued. If you, as the homeowner, are issued the building permit for a garage addition, you are responsible for meeting the requirements of the applicable codes. If you hire an electrician to do the electrical work, have him obtain the electrical permit. This way he is contractually responsible for passing the electrical inspections. In addition, if his work creates problems later—such as a fire—he

City of Sierra Vista

CITY OF SIERRA VISTA

BUILDING PERMIT APPLICATION

The undersigned hereby requests permission to do, or have done, the following described building improvements at the address, as indicated. All work will be done in conformance with applicable codes.

DATE_____

PERMIT TO BE ISSUED TO _____PHONE_____

ADDRESS_____

CONSTRUCTION SITE_____BLOCK_____

LOT #_____SUBDIVISION_____PARCEL ID #_____

CONTRACTOR_____

PHONE_____STATE LICENSE #_____

DESCRIPTION OF WORK. THIS MUST BE COMPLIED WITH: Sketch or site plan must be included showing dimensions and distances to lot lines and existing structures (may use back of app.)

_____

_____

_____

_____

_____VALUATION_____

SIGNED_____
             (Applicant)

- - - - - - - - - - - - - - - FOR OFFICE USE ONLY - - - - - - - - - - - - - - - -

ZONE_____BUILDING PERMIT FEE_____

SEWER CONNECT FEE_____PLAN CHECK FEE_____DISPOSAL FEE_____

APPROVED_____DISAPPROVED_____REASON_____

_____

_____

_____

_____

BUILDING INSPECTOR_____

Fig. 9-1. A typical building permit application (courtesy of the City of Sierra Vista, Arizona).

BUILDING PERMIT

PERMIT IS HEREBY GRANTED TO COVER THE WORK HEREINAFTER DESCRIBED. IN ACCORDANCE WITH THE BUILDING, PLUMBING, ELECTRICAL CODES AND OTHER EFFECTIVE ORDINANCES OF THE CITY OF SIERRA VISTA. THE PROPOSED WORK TO BE EXECUTED IN CONFORMITY WITH SAID LAWS. THE GRANTING OF THIS PERMIT DOES NOT ABROGATE OR ANNUL ANY DEED RESTRICTIONS OR OTHER LEGAL COVENANTS, AND GRANTS NO CONDITIONS IN EXCESS OF WHAT THE ORDINANCES PERMIT.

CITY OF SIERRA VISTA, ARIZONA

BUILDING PERMIT NO. № 408

PERMIT ISSUED TO: ____________

LOCATION OF PREMISES: ____________

LOT NUMBER: ____________

SUBDIVISION: ____________

DATE: ____________

CITY OF SIERRA VISTA ARIZONA

BUILDING	MISCELLANEOUS
NEW CONSTRUCTION ______	MOBILE HOME INSTALLATION ______
ADDITION ______	SIDEWALK / DRIVE ______
ALTERATION / REPAIR ______	POOL / SPA ______
DEMOLITION ______	SIGN ______
PATIO / COVER ______	RE-ROOF ______
SHED ______	PORCH / CARPORT ENCLOSURE ______
FENCE / WALL ______	FIREPLACE / STOVE ______
SEWER / SEPTIC ______	OTHER ______

GENERAL DESCRIPTION OF WORK ____________

CONTRACTOR: ____________
VALUATION: ____________
BUILDING PERMIT FEE: ____________
SEWER/SEPTIC PERMIT FEE: ____________
SEWER/SEPTIC PERMIT NO.: ____________
PLAN CHECK FEE: ____________

APPROVED BY ____________
CITY INSPECTOR

CITY OF SIERRA VISTA
COCHISE COUNTY, ARIZONA

Fig. 9-2. A typical building permit (courtesy of the City of Sierra Vista Arizona).

```
POST THIS CARD AT OR NEAR FRONT OF BUILDING

CITY OF SIERRA VISTA BUILDING DEPARTMENT

I N S P E C T I O N     R E C O R D


BUILDING PERMIT NO. _____

PERMIT ISSUED TO: _____

LOCATION OF PREMISES: _____

LOT NUMBER: _____

SUBDIVISION: _____

DATE: _____
```

INSPECTION	DATE	INITIAL
FOUNDATION:		
Setback		
Trench		
Reinforcing		
Compaction		
CONCRETE SLAB FLOOR:		
Electrical (Groundwork)		
Plumbing (Waste)		
Plumbing (Copper)		
Plumbing (Water Line)		
Plumbing (Sewer Tap)		
Septic Tank Location		
Rough Electrical		
Service Entry (Underground)		
Service Entry (Overhead)		
Rough Gas Piping		
Gas Pressure Check		
Heating & Ventilation		
Framing		
ROOFING:		
Sheathing		
Underlayment		
Flashing		
Shingle		
Tile		
Gravel		
FINAL:		
Address Posted		
Venting		
Glass & Glazing		
G.F.C.I.		
T. & P. Valve		
Combustion Air		
Fire Doors		
JOB COMPLETED		
CERTIFICATE OF OCCUPANCY		

Fig. 9-3. A typical building inspection record card (courtesy of the City of Sierra Vista, Arizona).

might be liable for the damage (depending on various circumstances). This applies to any specialty contractor or subcontractor you might hire.

Building departments, building officials, and municipalities are generally immune to any liability in connection to damage suits resulting from faulty construction, in spite of their authority and responsibility. You have no legal recourse against them should problems arise.

BUILDING INSPECTIONS

Once you have purchased building, plumbing, mechanical, and electrical permits, inspections are inevitable. The inspections will normally follow an order similar to this:

☐ Footings Inspection.
☐ Framing Inspection.
☐ Mechanical Rough-in Inspection.
☐ Plumbing Rough-in Inspection.
☐ Electrical Rough-in Inspection.
☐ Close-in Inspection.
☐ Final Mechanical Inspection.
☐ Final Plumbing Inspection.
☐ Final Electrical Inspection.
☐ Final Building Inspection.
☐ Issue of Occupancy Permit.

The inspections might vary somewhat in order and type from one locale to another, but basic requirements remain the same.

A record of the completed inspections is kept at the construction site and also at the building department. A typical building inspection card is shown in Fig. 9-3. Some building departments issue color-coded pass and fail slips that are affixed to the building permit. In either event, each time an inspection is held, the building inspector will verify that all previous inspections have been passed by examining your copy of the card or slips.

The footings inspection is held after the excavation is complete and all concrete forms and reinforcements are in place, but before the foundation is laid.

The framing inspection is conducted once the subfloor, all framing, wall, and roof sheathing is in place, but before the installation of roofing, siding, doors, windows, and mechanical, electrical, or plumbing work.

The rough-in inspections of mechanical, electrical, and plumbing work are made once all ductwork, pipes, and wires are installed in the framing, but before the walls are covered on the inside of the structure.

The close-in inspection is made after the rough-in inspections have been passed. The close-in inspection allows you to install the drywall, doors, windows, roofing, siding, and other items that will bring the structure to a finished state.

The final mechanical, plumbing, and electrical inspections are conducted after all of the respective fixtures are in place, and no other work is required to complete the installations. Depending on your local building department, these finals might be held either before or after the utilities are connected.

The final building inspection is conducted once the structure is ready to be moved into. The purpose of the final inspection is to verify that all previous inspections have been passed and to check all work completed since the close-in inspection was held. Once the final inspection is passed, an occupancy permit may be issued.

BUILDING INSPECTORS

Building inspectors have been some of the most helpful people I have known. I have spent countless hours on the phone and at construction sites asking these people questions and learning from them. Your building inspectors are intimately familiar with the content and interpretation of the building codes. They are aware of the most current and acceptable building materials and methods.

When the building inspector comes to your home, he is not bent on flunking you. He won't check to see how many nails you have bent, or laugh at the one or two cuts you made a little less than square. The inspector will check for things such as the proper lumber grades, stud or joist spacing, nail size and spacing, and other technical details of this type.

The inspector is on your side. When he comes

to your home, talk to him. More important is that you listen to him. Ask questions. Offer him some coffee. The building inspectors I have dealt with have always been friendly, cheerful, and full of ideas. Listen carefully to any suggestions an inspector offers. The building inspector can almost always show you a better way of doing something. Remember, you have purchased the professional services of this person with your building permit. Take advantage of it.

If the building inspector does fail you on an inspection, he will gladly tell you how to correct any problems that exist. Normally, you are allowed one reinspection of each type (footings, framing, etc.), with no additional fee. Often the inspector will pass you in spite of a minor discrepancy that might exist, providing you solemnly promise to fix it before he returns for the next inspection. If the inspector gives you such a break, keep your promise. Violation of this trust will only make your future inspections tougher. The inspector never forgets.

I spoke with a senior building inspector prior to writing this chapter and asked what advice he would give concerning drywall construction. Here is pretty much what he said:

"Make sure that the wall sheets are pushed up tightly under the edges of the ceiling sheets. Don't just stand them up against the studs and nail them in place. Make sure that the holes in the wall studs for electrical wires are far enough away from the stud edges so you don't accidentally drive a nail through a wire. Drywall any area where a fire hazard might exist. I know of two identical structures in this area, both of which had fires in their storage rooms. In one of these buildings, the storage room was constructed with a one-hour gypsum firewall. The other was not. The building with the firewall sustained $500 in damage, most of which was confined to the contents of the storage room only. The other building went up like a match. The fire spread from the storage room and caused $50,000 in damage."

That sounds like good advice to me. If there is any doubt in your mind as to whether or not you need a building permit, or what codes you must comply with, ask your local building inspector. He knows what codes have been adopted by your municipality and what supplements they may have added to them.

Appendix
Framing Diagrams and Tables

The quality and appearance of a finished drywall system can be affected by the framing of the structure to which it is applied. Contained in this Appendix are diagrams (Figs. A-1 through A-9) of accepted framing practices.

Also contained in this Appendix are framing tables (Tables A-1 through A-6) for ceiling joists and wall studs. The joist spans in the ceiling joist tables were computed for Douglas Fir framing lumber graded #2 by the National Lumber Grading Authority (NLGA) at 19 percent moisture content. It should be noted that the values in the tables will vary based on lumber species, grade, grading agency, and moisture content. The values in the stud table are constant for all lumber types graded #3, STUD, or better.

		Joist Spacing		
		12" oc	16" oc	24" oc
Joist size	2×4	12'8"	11'6"	10'0"
	2×6	19'11"	18'1"	15'6"
	2×8	26'2"	23'10"	20'5"
	2×10	33'5"	30'5"	26'0"

Table A-1. Maximum Allowable Spans for Ceiling Joists Supporting a Gypsum Ceiling with no Attic or Floor Above, Based on 10-pounds per Square Foot Live Load.

130

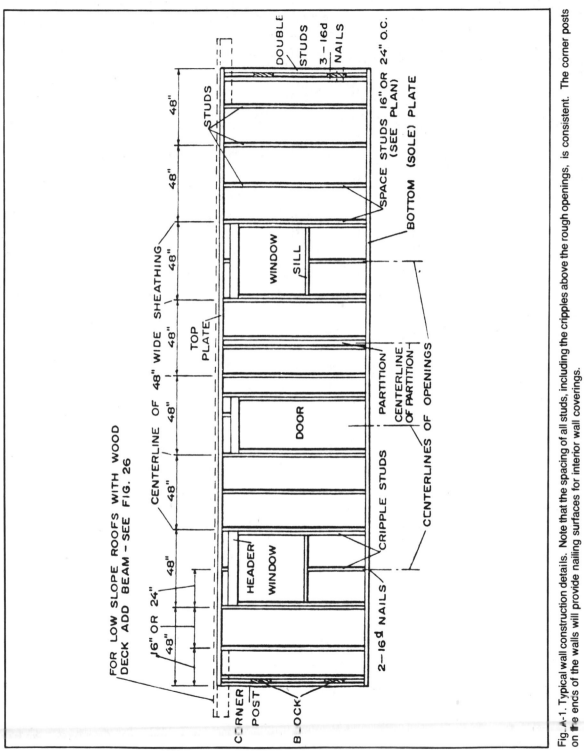

Fig. A-1. Typical wall construction details. Note that the spacing of all studs, including the cripples above the rough openings, is consistent. The corner posts on the ends of the walls will provide nailing surfaces for interior wall coverings.

131

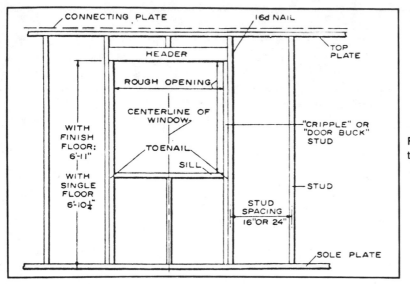

Fig. A-2. Construction details of a typical rough opening.

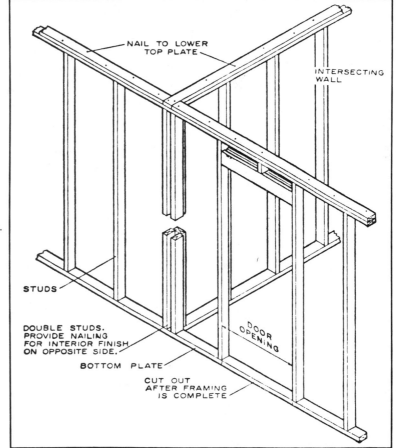

Fig. A-3. Details of wall intersection. Note the fastening of the double plates.

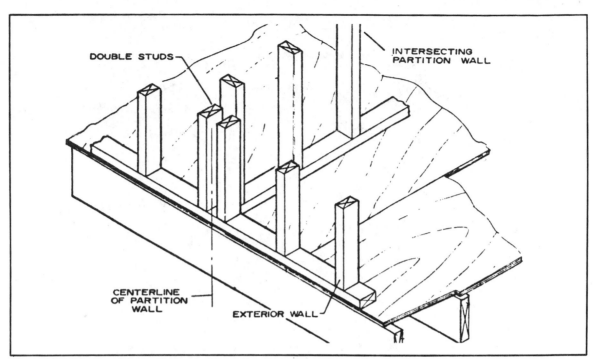

Fig. A-4. Wall intersection detail. The double studs will provide nailing surfaces for interior wall coverings.

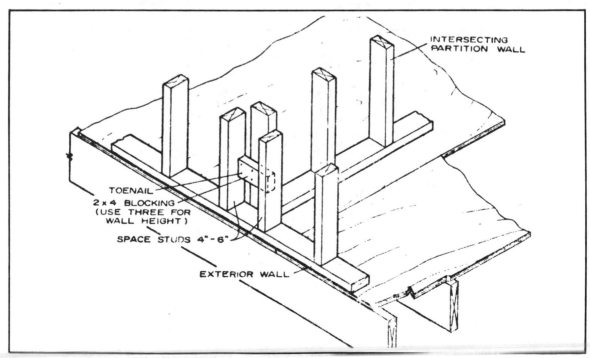

Fig. A-5. Alternate method of wall intersection.

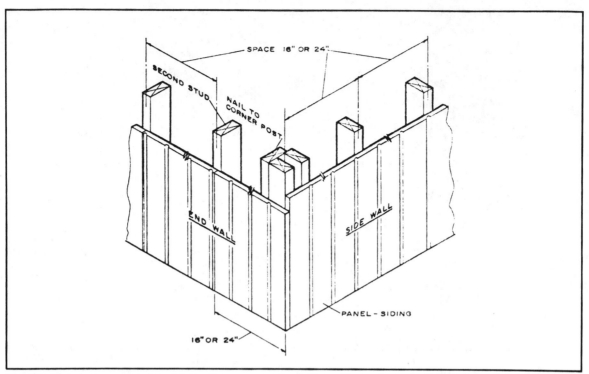

Fig. A-6. Wall corner construction details. The corner post provides nailing surfaces for the interior wall covering.

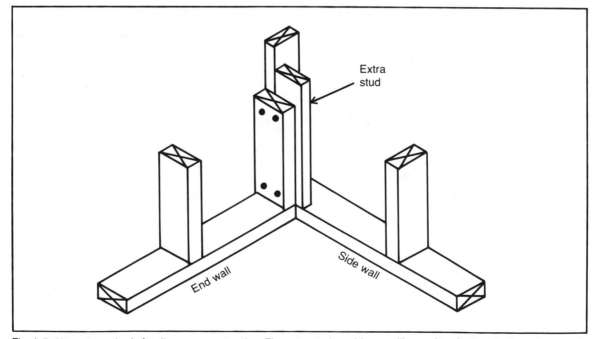

Fig. A-7. Alternate method of wall corner construction. The extra stud provides a nailing surface for the interior wall covering.

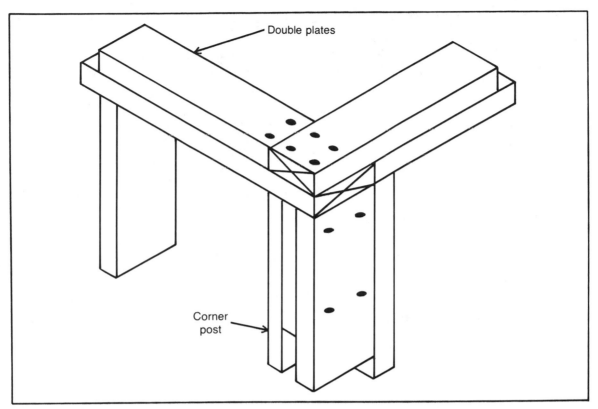

Fig. A-8. Intersection of wall corner at top of wall. Note the nailing pattern in the double plates.

Joist size		Joist Spacing		
		12" oc	16" oc	24" oc
	2×4	10'0"	9'1"	7'6"
	2×6	15'16"	13'5"	10'10"
	2×8	20'5"	17'9"	14'3"
	2×10	26'0"	22'7"	18'3"

Table A-2. Maximum Allowable Spans for Ceiling Joists Supporting a Gypsum Ceiling with Limited Attic Space above Where Development of Future Rooms is not Possible, Based on 20-pounds per Square Foot Live Load.

Table A-3. A Maximum Allowable Spans for Ceiling (Floor) Joists Supporting a Gypsum Ceiling and a Floor of a Habitable Room Above, Based on 40-pounds per Square Foot Live Load.

Joist size		Joist Spacing		
		12" oc	16" oc	24" oc
	2×6	10'11"	9'11"	8'6"
	2×8	14'5"	13'1"	11'3"
	2×10	18'5"	16'9"	14'4"
	2×12	22'5"	20'4"	17'5"

Load Bearing Walls	2×4's*at 16" oc
Non Load Bearing Walls	2×4's at 24" oc 2×3's at 16" oc

Table A-4. Stud Spacing for
Structure of Three Stories or Less in Height.

*For 1st floor of 3-floor structure stud must be 2×6 or ×3

Table A-5. Lumber Size Chart.

ITEM	THICKNESSES			FACE WIDTHS		
	NOMINAL	Minimum Dressed		NOMINAL	Minimum Dressed	
		Dry[6]	Green[6]		Dry[6]	Green[6]
		Inches	Inches		Inches	Inches
Boards[7]	1 1¼ 1½	¾ 1 1¼	$^{25}\!/_{32}$ $1^{1}\!/_{32}$ $1^{9}\!/_{32}$	2 3 4 5 6 7 8 9 10 11 12 14 16	1½ 2½ 3½ 4½ 5½ 6½ 7¼ 8¼ 9¼ 10¼ 11¼ 13¼ 15¼	$1^{9}\!/_{16}$ $2^{9}\!/_{16}$ $3^{9}\!/_{16}$ 4⅝ 5⅝ 6⅝ 7½ 8½ 9½ 10½ 11½ 13½ 15½
Dimension	2	1½	$1^{9}\!/_{16}$	2 3 4 5	1½ 2½ 3½ 4½	$1^{9}\!/_{16}$ $2^{9}\!/_{16}$ $3^{9}\!/_{16}$ 4⅝
Dimension	2½ 3 3½	2 2½ 3	$2^{1}\!/_{16}$ $2^{9}\!/_{16}$ $3^{1}\!/_{16}$	6 8 10 12 14 16	5½ 7¼ 9¼ 11¼ 13¼ 15¼	5⅝ 7½ 9½ 11½ 13½ 15½
Dimension	4 4½	3½ 4	$3^{9}\!/_{16}$ $4^{1}\!/_{16}$	2 3 4 5 6 8 10 12 14 16	1½ 2½ 3½ 4½ 5½ 7¼ 9¼ 11¼	$1^{9}\!/_{16}$ $2^{9}\!/_{16}$ $3^{9}\!/_{16}$ 4⅝ 5⅝ 7½ 9½ 11½ 13½ 15½
Timbers	5 & Thicker		½ Off	5 & Wider		½ Off

[6] "Dry" lumber has been dried to 19 percent moisture content or less; "green" lumber has a moisture content of more than 19 percent.

[7] Boards less than the minimum thickness for 1 inch nominal but ⅝ inch or greater thickness dry (11/16 inch green) may be regarded as American Standard Lumber, but such boards shall be marked to show the size and condition of seasoning at the time of dressing. They shall also be distinguished from 1-inch boards on invoices and certificates.

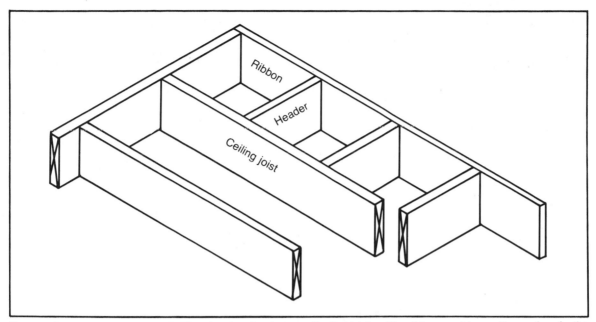

Fig. A-9. Ceiling construction details. The short headers between the first joint and the ribbon provide a nailing surface for the wallboard edge.

Table A-6. Nail Size Chart for Common Nails. Dimensions Will Vary with Nail Type (e.g., Box, Finishing, Drywall).

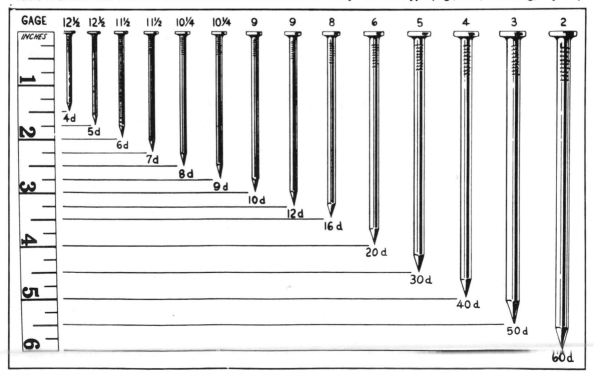

Glossary

all-purpose joint compound—A joint compound combining the best features of taping and topping compounds; used for all coats on drywall joints.

angle sander—A sanding pad with two sanding planes meeting at a right angle; used for sanding inside corner joints in drywall construction.

annular-ringed nail—Any nail having ringed grooves in its shank to increase holding power.

backing side—The side of a gypsum wallboard covered with coarse gray paper which contacts the framing members of the structure.

baseboard—A wide molding attached to a wall where the wall meets the floor.

butt joint—An untapered joint formed by the flush edges on the ends of adjacent gypsum wallboards.

calcination—The process by which the chemically combined water in gypsum rock and gypsum wallboard is driven off as steam by heat.

caulking gun—A tool used to apply caulking, adhesives, and sealants contained in 11-ounce or 29-ounce tubular cartridges.

ceiling joist—A horizontal framing member which provides form and support for a ceiling without a floor above.

cement-coated nail—Any nail coated with a dry cement that increases its holding power.

circle cutter—A tool used like a compass to score the face paper of gypsum wallboard to cut round holes.

corner bead—A galvanized metal strip with two flanges meeting at a right angle and a rounded edge; used for reinforcing and forming outside corners in drywall construction.

corner post—The first or last vertical framing member in a wall, usually made of two studs separated by blocks, providing additional rigidity and nailing surfaces for interior wall coverings.

corner trowel—A joint knife with a blade folded at a right angle used to fill and finish inside corner joints in drywall construction.

cratering—The forming of small depressions or craters in joint compound as it is applied due to air bubbles or overly thick joint compound.

cripple stud—A short wall stud located above or below a rough opening; it supports a header or plate.

crown—The curvature of a drywall joint; neccessary for blending of the joint into the wallboard surface.

curved joint trowel—A joint finishing trowel having a curved blade; used to create the proper crown in joints during finishing.

d—A symbol indicating nail size, once indicating the price of 100 nails in English pence.

dimple—The depression created around a nailhead during nailing in drywall construction that allows the nailhead to be covered with joint compound.

double nailing—A method of nailing gypsum wallboard characterized by nails 2 to 2½ inches apart placed in pairs 12 inches apart.

double plate—The top horizontal framing member of a wall, usually constructed of two pieces of 2×4.

drying-type joint compound—Drywall joint compound that cures by air drying in an amount of time dependent on temperature and relative humidity.

drywall—Any interior wall covering, particularly gypsum wallboard, that is applied to the framing of a structure in a dry state in contrast to materials such as plaster.

drywall construction adhesive—An adhesive packaged in 11-ounce or 29-ounce cartridges designed to fasten gypsum wallboard to wood; it's applied with a caulking gun.

drywall nail—A steel nail between 1¼ and 2⅛ inches long with a head 19/64 inch wide and a shank of #12, 13, or 14 American wire gauge in thickness with either annular rings or a cement coating on the shank; used for fastening gypsum wallboard to studs and joists.

dust mask—A paper or felt mask worn over the face during sanding or painting to protect the lungs from floating particles.

expanding wall anchor—A device used to attach fixtures to gypsum wallboard characterized by a shank that expands behind the back of the wallboard during tightening.

exterior ceiling board—A type of gypsum wallboard with a sag-resistant core and moisture-resistant paper jacket; used to finish ceilings in outdoor applications.

exterior wall—The outside wall surface of a structure.

feathered edge—The thinly tapered edge of a coat of joint compound created during finishing to blend the joint into the wallboard surface.

filler coat—The initial coat of joint compound and tape applied to a drywall joint for the purpose of structural bonding.

finish coat—The final coat of joint compound applied to a drywall joint for cosmetic purposes.

finish side—The side of a gypsum wallboard covered with smooth Manila paper intended for decoration as the interior wall surface of the structure; also the side on which the wallboard edges are tapered.

Fire Resistance Design Manual—A publication of the Gypsum Association which specifies the fire resistance ratings of various gypsum wallboard installations.

floor joist—A horizontal framing member which provides form and support for the floors of a structure, and in some cases, a ceiling below.

framing—The assembly of the studs, joists, plates, sills, rafters, headers, and other members of a structure which provide form and support for the structure.

furring—Strips of wood or metal applied over the framing or wall and ceiling surfaces of a structure to provide a base for a new wall or ceiling surface.

gypsum—Calcium sulfate, a white mineral containing chemically combined water, used in the manufacture of plaster, fertilizer, and gypsum wallboard.

Gypsum Association—A trade association composed of gypsum product manufacturers.

gypsum wallboard—Noncombustible interior wall covering in the form of sheets ranging in thickness of ¼ to ⅝ inch and lengths of 6 to 16 feet with a standard width of 4 feet having a gypsm core and a heavy paper jacket.

habitable room—As defined in most building codes, any room meeting the requirements of sleeping, living, cooking, or dining, excluding closets, pantries, hallways, bathrooms, laundries, storage spaces, utility rooms, and similar spaces.

hardening-type joint compound—Any drywall joint compound that chemically hardens in a set amount of time regardless of its moisture content; always produced in powdered form.

header—A horizontal framing member, usually doubled in thickness, that supports the vertical load over a rough opening.

horizontal coursing—A superior method of drywall construction characterized by gypsum wallboards fastened to the walls with the long dimension in a horizontal position.

interior wall—The inside wall surface of a structure.

inside corner—A drywall corner joint formed by two surfaces meeting at an angle smaller than 180°, such as the joint where a wall and ceiling meet.

joint—The seam formed by the unfinished edges of adjacent gypsum wallboards in drywall construction.

joint cement—See joint compound.

joint compound—A white, pastelike compound resembling plaster that is applied to drywall joints for structural and cosmetic effects. See also all-purpose joint compound, drying-type joint compound, hardening-type joint compound, taping compound, and topping compound.

joint finishing—The process of reinforcing and disguising drywall joints with joint tape and joint compound.

joint knife—A tool resembling a putty knife having a blade between 6 inches and 24 inches wide; used to apply joint compound to drywall joints.

joint staggering—A superior method of drywall construction characterized by the butt joints occurring at the ends of the wallboards being offset by 4 feet so as not to occur on the same stud or joist.

joint tape—Paper tape without adhesive, usually 2½ inches wide, used to reinforce drywall joints. Some joint tapes are perforated with holes for additional structural bonding.

joist—See floor joist and ceiling joist.

keyhole saw—A handsaw having a pointed blade between 8 and 18 inches long, used for punching and cutting holes.

load-bearing wall—A wall which supports the weight of a floor or roof above.

molly bolt—See toggle bolt.

mud—A widely used and professionally accepted slang term for drywall joint compound. See joint compound.

mud pan—A rectangular tray usually 12 inches long, 4 inches wide, and 5 inches deep used for applying joint compound with a joint knife during drywall construction.

nailer—A block or strip attached to a framing member of a structure for the sole purpose of providing a nailing surface for wall covering materials.

National Electrical Code—A code published by the National Fire Protection Association which describes acceptable electrical installations in all structures.

nonload-bearing wall—A wall which supports no weight other than its own.

o.c.—Abbreviation for on center.

on center—A term used to indicate the distance from the center of one framing member or fastener to the next. Also means same as center to center.

One & Two Family Dwelling Code—A building code published jointly by the American Insurance Association, Building Officials And Code Administrators International Inc., the International Conference of Building Officials, and the Southern Building Code Congress International covering construction standards for one and two-family detached dwellings of less than three stories in height.

orphan—A small particle of dried joint compound which has fallen into a container of fresh joint compound.

outside corner joint—A drywall joint formed by two surfaces which meet at an angle greater than 180°, such as the joint formed at the side of a doorway.

partition wall—A wall which divides the interior space of a structure into separate rooms. Partition walls may be load bearing or nonload bearing.

penny—Term for nail size abbreviated by the symbol d. See d.

perimeter wall—The wall enclosing the perimeter of a structure, almost always load bearing, sometimes mistakenly referred to as an exterior wall. See exterior wall.

plaster board—Another name for gypsum wallboard.

pole sander—A flat sanding pad attached to a broom handle by a universal joint; used for sanding drywall joints.

rafter—A framing member usually placed on an angle which provides form and support for a roof and in some cases a ceiling also.

razor knife—See utility knife.

respirator—See dust mask.

ring-shanked nail—See annular-ringed nail.

rough framing—See framing.

rough-in—The installation of framing, wiring, plumbing, and ductwork prior to covering the interior walls and ceilings of a structure.

rough-in inspection—The required building inspection of any rough-in installations prior to covering the interior walls and ceilings of a structure.

rough opening—An opening in the framing of a structure designed to accommodate a fixture such as a door or window.

scab—See nailer.

soffit—The finished surface on the underside of an eave or overhang.

Sheetrock—A trade name of the United States Gypsum Company often misused as a common name for gypsum wallboard in general.

Sheetrock knife—See utility knife.

Sheetrock nail—See drywall nail.

shore—See T brace.

sole plate—The bottom horizontal framing member of a wall; used to attach the studs to the subfloor.

spackle—See joint compound.

stippled surface—A type of pattern created in ceiling textures by poking the applied texture with a brush.

stud—A vertical framing member in the wall of a structure which provides form and support for the wall.

studfinder—A magnetic or electronic device used to locate the studs and joists in a finished drywall system.

subfloor—The rough floor surface of a structure, usually covered with plywood and in some cases particleboard also.

T brace—A tall brace shaped like the letter T used to hold gypsum wallboards to the ceiling joists during nailing.

T square—A drywalling square 4 feet long and 2 feet wide shaped like the letter T; used for measuring and cutting gypsum wallboard.

taping compound—A type of drywall joint finishing compound used only for filler coats; provides high structural bonding.

textured ceiling—A ceiling coated with a material such as joint compound and finsihed in an uneven or raised pattern.

toggle bolt—A bolt assembly used to fasten fixtures to hollow wall surfaces having a spring-loaded wing assembly that expands once it is inserted into the wall cavity.

topping compound—A type of drywall joint compound used for second and finish coats only; provides easy finishing with little structural bonding.

top plate—The top horizontal member of a wall; same as a double plate but not doubled. See double plate.

trimmer stud—A wall stud that provides support for the sides of a rough opening and placed parallel to a cripple stud.

type-X wallboard—A gypsum wallboard with a specially treated fire resistant core that provides additional fire resistance, usually no less than 45 minutes.

Uniform Building Code—A building code published by the International Conference of Building Officials setting forth the structural requirements for most structures occupied by people.

Uniform Mechanical Code—A building code published jointly by the International Conference of Building Officials and the International Association of Plumbing and Mechanical Officials describing acceptable installation practices for heating, cooling, ventilation, and associated fixtures in structures occupied by people.

Uniform Plumbing Code—A building code published by the International Association of Plumbing and Mechanical Officials describing acceptable plumbing fixture installations in structures occupied by people.

utility knife—A knife with a short, sharp, replaceable blade used for scoring the face paper of gypsum wallboards during cutting.

valley joint—A joint formed by the tapered edges of adjacent gypsum wallboards having a valley in which joint tape is embedded with joint compound.

vapor barrier—A moisture-resistant membrane placed behind a wall or ceiling to prevent moisture inside the structure from entering the wall cavity and condensing into water.

vertical coursing—A method of drywall construction characterized by gypsum wallboard applied to the walls of a structure with the long dimension in a vertical position.

wall anchor—See expanding wall anchor.

wallboard—Any interior wall covering applied in the form of large sheets, such as gypsum wallboard.

water-resistant joint compound—A type of joint compound that resists moisture penetration; used to seal and finish the joints of water-resistant gypsum wallboard installations.

water-resistant wallboard—A type of gypsum wallboard with an asphalt composition core and a specially treated water-resistant paper jacket; used in places where high moisture conditions prevail, such as in kitchens and bathrooms.

Index

Index

A

Adhesive, 15
Adhesive, drywall construction, 139
Anchors, wall, 109

B

Baseboard, 138
Bench, drywalling, 29
Board sag, 91
Bolts, toggle, 109-110
Bonding, 10-11
Bonding agents, 13
Building codes, 34, 123
Building inspection, 127
Building inspections, 123, 128
Building inspectors, 128
Building permit application, typical, 125
Building permit, typical, 126
Building permits, 123-124
Butt joint, 85, 138

C

Calcination, 138
Catering, 139
Caulking gun, 15, 99, 100
Ceiling board, 6

Ceiling board, exterior, 139
Ceiling construction details, 137
Ceiling coverage, 55
Ceiling joist, 138
Ceiling joists, 54
Ceiling spans, 135
Ceiling texture, 116, 118
Ceiling, drywalling the, 49
Ceilings, textured, 115
Cement-coated nails, 15
Channels, 14
Circle cutter, 18, 51, 138
Code, mechanical, 124
Codes, building, 34, 123
Compound topping, 8, 142
Compound, all-purpose, 8
Compound, drying, 8
Compound, hardening, 8
Compound, joint, 8, 22, 35, 66
Compound, powdered, 8
Compound, pre-mixed, 8
Compound, taping, 8
Compound, water-resistant joint, 142
Compounds, joint, 8-9
Compounds, taping, 9
Construction adhesive, drywall, 139
Corner bead, 61, 73-74, 79, 138
Corner bead, tapping, 63
Corner beads, 78

Corner beads, three most popular, 14
Corner joint, 84-85
Corner post, 138
Corner trowel, 138
Corners, reinforcing, 62
Coursing, horizontal, 57
Cracking, angle, 91
Cracking, bead, 91
Cracking, field, 91
Crown, 139
Curved surfaces, drywalling, 59

D

Dimple, 139
Discoloration, 92
Door arch, 60
Drywall, 139
Drywall construction adhesive, 15, 139
Drywall coverage, 35
Drywall estimating, 33
Drywall estimating guide, 37
Drywall fastening requirements, 34
Drywall joints, 22-23
Drywall joints, sanding, 24
Drywall materials, 1
Drywall nail, 139
Drywall nails, 15

Drywall problems, checklist for, 92
Drywall repairs, 87
Drywall saw, 21
Drywall systems, defective, 89
Drywall utility saw, 19
Drywalling curved surfaces, 59
Drywalling hammer, 27
Drywalling projects, large, 37
Drywalling the ceiling, 48
Drywalling tools, 17
Dust mask, 27, 77, 139

E

Electrical box, 41, 52, 68
Electrical boxes, cutting around, 17

F

Fastener imperfections, 90
Fastener requirements, 34
Fasteners, 96, 105
Fasteners, bulges around, 105
Fasteners, gypsum wallboard, 15
Feathered edge, 139
Filler coat, 139
Filler coat, applying the, 67
Finish coat, 139
Finish coat, applying the, 81
Finish side, 139
Finish, discoloration of, 106
Finish, gloss paint, 106
Finish, joint darkening, 106
Finish, shadowing, 106
Finishing tools, joint, 19
Finishing, joint, 65
Fire Resistance Design Manual, 139
Fixtures, mounting, 108
Floor joist, 139
Framing, 93, 139
Framing diagrams and tables, 130
Framing member, 94
Framing protrusions, 95
Furring, 139

G

Glue, 34
Glue, applying, 53
Gluing patterns, 54
Gypsum, 1, 3, 139
Gypsum Association, 140
Gypsum panels, 7
Gypsum sheathing, 7
Gypsum wallboard, 2, 5-7, 29, 58, 88-89, 140
Gypsum wallboard application, 38
Gypsum wallboard fasteners, 15
Gypsum wallboard requirements, 33
Gypsum wallboard thicknesses, 16

Gypsum wallboard, cutting, 45-46, 48
Gypsum wallboard, nailing, 40, 55
Gypsum wallboard, scoring, 51
Gypsum wallboard, snapping, 46, 50

H

Hammer, 113
Hammer handle, rubber, 63
Hammer, drywalling, 27
Header, 140
Horizontal coursing, 57, 140

J

Jigsaw, single-speed electric, 52
Joint, 140
Joint cement, 140
Joint compound, 10, 22, 66, 69, 71, 75, 83, 140
Joint compound, all-purpose, 138
Joint compound, drying, 139
Joint compound, hardening, 140
Joint compound, water-resistant, 142
Joint compounds, 8, 26
Joint cracking, 91
Joint defects, 90
Joint filler, 76
Joint finishing, 65, 140
Joint finishing tools, 19
Joint finishing trowel, 24
Joint knife, 18, 74-75, 140
Joint reinforcement requirements, 34
Joint reinforcements, 10
Joint staggering, 140
Joint tape, 69-70, 72, 76, 83, 140
Joint tape, paper, 11, 72
Joint, butt, 82, 85, 138
Joint, corner, 75, 84
Joint, outside corner, 140
Joint, valley, 83, 142
Joints, 104
Joints, angle cracking,
Joints, blisters in tape, 102
Joints, butt, 55-56
Joints, center cracking, 103
Joints, edge cracking, 103
Joist, 140
Joists and studs, finding, 111

K

Knife, joint, 74-75
Knife, joint finishing, 23
Knife, razor, 141
Knife, taping, 22
Knife, utility, 18, 45, 142
Knives, joint, 66

M

Mask, dust, 26-27, 139
Mastic, 5
Materials, drywall, 1
Materials, estimating, 33
Materials, texturing, 115
Mud, 70, 86, 121, 140
Mud pan, 25
Mud, applying the second coat of, 76

N

Nail holds, 97
Nail size, 137
Nail sizes, 16
Nail, annular-ringed, 138
Nail, cement-coated, 138
Nail, drywall, 139
Nailer, 140
Nailhead finder, 30
Nailhead, dimpled, 43
Nailheads, 22, 66-67, 71, 83-84, 113
Nailing pattern, 135
Nailing pattern for butt joints, 56
Nailing pattern for gypsum wallboard, 55
Nailing pattern, recommended, 63
Nailing wallboard, 60
Nailing, double, 139
Nails, 34, 40, 42, 49, 96, 105
Nails, cement-coated, 15
Nails, drywall, 15
Nails, selector guide for, 16
Nails, unseated, 98
National Electrical Code, 124, 140

O

On center, 140
One & Two Family Dwelling Code, 141
Orphan, 141

P

Paint roller, 117
Panels, board sagging in, 106
Panels, damaged edges on, 93
Panels, improperly fitted, 95
Panels, loose, 91
Panels, loosely fastened, 98
Panels, surface fractured after application, 99
Panels, water-damaged, 93
Penny, 140-141
Pipe outlet reinforcements, paper, 12
Plaster, 1
Plumbing code, 123

Pole sander, 25

R

Racking, bead, 91
Repairs, drywall, 87
Roller-lifter, wallboard, 28

S

Sander, angle, 26, 80, 138
Sander, pole, 25, 77, 79, 140-141
Sanding, 77, 79-80
Sandpaper, 24
Saw, drywall utility, 19
Saw, keyhole, 52, 140
Saw, variable-speed electric reciprocating, 20
Sheetrock, 2, 141
Shim, using a, 44
Soffit, 141
Spackle, 141
Stud spacing, 136
Studfinder, 141, 113
Studfinder, electronic, 31, 114
Studfinder, magnetic, 30
Studs and joists, finding, 111
Surfaces, drywalling curved, 59

T

T brace, 29, 141
T square, 21, 45, 141

Tape, 6
Tape, joint, 69-70, 72, 76, 83
Tape, metal corner, 13
Tape, paper, 13
Tape, paper joint, 11
Taping knife, 22
Texture pattern, 118
Texture, applying the, 120
Texturing materials, 115
Texturing tools, 115
Time, estimating your, 33
Toggle bolts, 110, 141
Toggle bolts, installing spring-loaded, 109
Tools, cutting, 17
Tools, drywalling, 17,
Tools, joint finishing, 19
Tools, other useful, 26
Tools, texturing, 115
Trim, 14
Trowel, 23, 71, 76, 119
Trowel, corner, 138
Trowel, curved joint, 139
Trowel, joint finishing, 24
Trowel, notched, 121

U

Utility knife, 142

V

Valley joint, 142

Vapor barrier, 142
Vertical coursing, 142

W

Wall anchor, 111, 142
Wall anchor, expanding, 139
Wall anchors, installing expanding, 109
Wall construction details, typical, 131
Wall corner construction, 134
Wall intersection, 132-133
Wall joint, checking for smoothness, 78
Wall joint, feathered edge of a, 78
Wall studs, 113
Wall, exterior, 139
Wallboard, 1-2, 142
Wallboard application, gypsum, 38
Wallboard estimating guide, 37
Wallboard fasteners, gypsum, 15
Wallboard, cutting, 48
Wallboard, cutting gypsum, 45
Wallboard, gypsum, 2-7, 29, 33, 58, 88, 140
Wallboard, nailing gypsum, 40, 55
Wallboard, scoring, 51
Wallboard, snapping, 46, 50
Wallboard, water-resistant, 142
Water damage, 92

OTHER POPULAR TAB BOOKS OF INTEREST